T0248404

OBELISK ODYSSEY

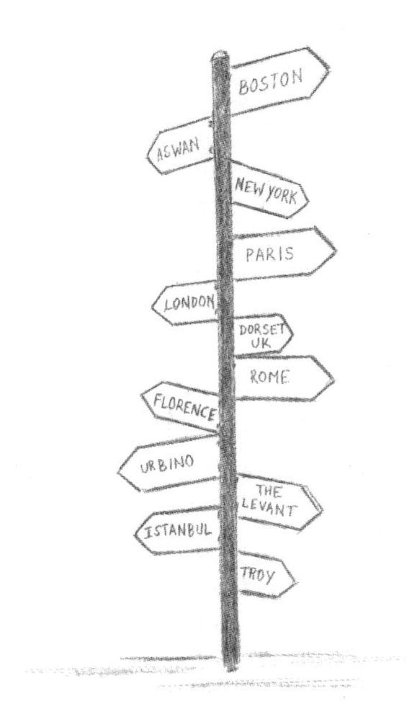

OBELISK ODYSSEY

stops along the way

www.amplifypublishinggroup.com

Obelisk Odyssey: 26 Ancient Monoliths, 4 Continents, and 1 Man's Monumental Search for Meaning

For more information, please contact:
Amplify Publishing, an imprint of Amplify Publishing Group
620 Herndon Parkway, Suite 220
Herndon, VA 20170
info@amplifypublishing.com

Library of Congress Control Number: 2024937961

CPSIA Code: PRV0624A

ISBN-13: 979-8-89138-259-6

Printed in the United States

To Eileen and the girls:

What a fabulous journey it's been with all of you.

With all my love.

The longer you can look back,
the farther you can look forward.

—Winston Churchill

I cannot rest from travel: I will drink
Life to the lees: All times I have enjoy'd
Greatly . . .
How dull it is to pause, to make an end,
To rust unburnish'd, not to shine in use!
As tho' to breathe were life!

—"Ulysses," ***Alfred Lord Tennyson***

OBELISK ODYSSEY

26 Ancient Monoliths, 4 Continents, and 1 Man's Monumental Search for Meaning

Mark Ciccone

With Illustrations by Eileen Keeney Ciccone

amplify

an imprint of Amplify Publishing Group

Contents

Part III
THE OBELISKS OF THE FORMER ROMAN EMPIRE: ITALY AND TURKEY

AUTHOR'S NOTE

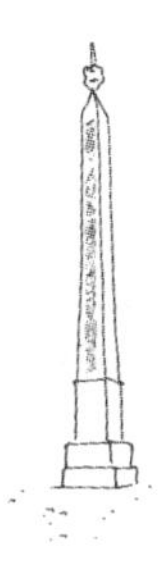

An obelisk is a tall, narrow, four-sided structure, typically with a square base that gradually tapers to its top. The summit is crowned by a pyramid-like top called a pyramidion. The word is derived from the Greek word *obeliskos*, which originally meant "skewer" or "spit."

There are many obelisks in the world today, but the oldest and most significant ones are Egyptian. Initially erected by pharaohs, they all have their origins in the granite quarries of the southern Egyptian town of Aswan. They are all single stones, or monoliths. The Egyptians referred to them as *tekenhu*, which meant "to pierce." Their shape was intended to depict a solid ray of sunlight pointing skyward, paying tribute to the gods and their earthly representative, the pharaoh.

There are only twenty-six Egyptian obelisks in the world today. Eleven are still in Egypt, and fifteen are in other countries. Italy has ten, England has two, and Turkey, the United States, and France have one each. With a presence on four continents, we can say that the Egyptian obelisk is the oldest man-made "product" with global distribution.

The Egyptians were not the only people to create obelisks. Other ancient civilizations, such as the Ethiopians, Phoenicians, and in particular the Romans, made their own too. But these come well after the Egyptians. Many are made of stone other than granite. Some are not monoliths. Some that were quarried in Aswan and stand today in Europe were never erected in Egypt at all. All such ancient obelisks are interesting, but they are outside the parameters of this book, which only focuses on the twenty-six Egyptian ones and my goal to see all of them.

One way to think about the Egyptian obelisks is that they have passed through three "life stages." The first was during the ancient era when they were originally erected in Egypt by the pharaohs. The second occurred when, for various reasons, they were later moved to their current locations (only six are still in their original Pharaonic positions). The third stage is their contemporary existence in those same locations, most of which have dramatically changed since the obelisks were first placed there. For example, the obelisks in New York, Paris, and London were moved from Egypt and erected in their current locations in the nineteenth century. But these locations have physically changed since then and reflect the values and aspirations of the modern societies in which they now stand. Although this book covers all three "life stages," it puts a bit more emphasis on the third, about which little has been written. It is here, in their current contexts, that these most ancient of all structures have something to say individually and collectively to a contemporary audience.

I have approached this not as an historian or an expert in Egyptology, which I am not, but rather as the "common man," a self-styled man of leisure trying to understand how the past meets the present and how it might meet the future. Hopefully, there's a spot for such a voice to be heard.

Prologue

CHARLESTOWN, MASSACHUSETTS, 1978: A MEMORY

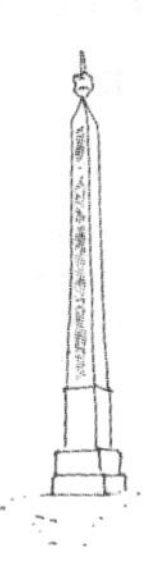

Not long after I had finished the travels that are described in this book, I was driving over a bridge just north of downtown Boston on my way to Vermont. As I glanced off to my right at the familiar and historic urban setting in the immediate vicinity, a memory that involved three people suddenly popped into my head. At first it took the form of a tableau—a motionless, faded image that had been tucked away and buried deep within my subconscious for more than a generation. With my mind now stimulated by the memory, the image gradually came to life, evolving into a vignette that had occurred long ago in the area I was now driving past. The day, the place, even some of the dialogue among the trio (or at least a reasonable approximation of it) began to fill in for me in surprising detail.

Picture this scene:

It is a blisteringly hot July day, and the young family of three is tired. They have driven an hour into Boston from their home in the suburbs. They are new to the area, the father having been transferred here two months previously. They are in the city to see the historic parts of their new hometown.

They have just visited the Revolutionary War era ship USS *Constitution* (a.k.a. "Old Ironsides") and are now walking through an old neighborhood, following the red line etched into the sidewalk, called the Freedom Trail, which connects pedestrians to many of the historic spots in Boston. The mother is pushing a stroller, and the little girl inside is becoming fidgety. Although she's very precocious, the child is far too young to appreciate the sights, but the parents plunge on in the intense heat. Suddenly the mother stops and points at a structure ahead.

"Oh, look at that big thing there!" she exclaims, pointing at a concrete towerlike structure in front of them. She is trying to engage her young daughter, who has been pleading to go home.

"It's the Bunker Hill Monument. It's a really important part of our history," chimes in the father. He is also doing his best to drill some unwanted history into his firstborn's head, which, at this time, has swiveled nearly 180 degrees away from the monument in order to look at two dogs frolicking in the grass.

They soon arrive at the monument and join a little tour led by a national park ranger. He is giving the background of the famous battle that occurred here in 1775.

"It was an important moment for this country," he explains. "Even though it was technically a victory for the British, the colonists put up a great fight. It showed they could hold their own against the greatest army in the world. It inspired all the colonies. Some years later some prominent local citizens decided to commemorate this spot with a monument. There was a contest, and designers and architects were asked to submit their ideas. One submission came from an unknown twenty-two-year-old Harvard student named Horatio Greenough, who had visited Italy and had fallen in love with the Egyptian obelisks he saw there. They are some of the most famous and historically important structures ever built, and he thought the US should have one. His sketches won approval, and so that's why this monument is in the form of an obelisk. Here's what he said." The guide takes out a sheet of paper and reads:

> *The obelisk has, to my eye, a singular aptitude in its form and character to call attention to a spot memorable in history. It says but one word. But it speaks loud. Here!* *[1]

"Do you know what that means?" the guide asks the little girl.

She stares back, eyes frozen, slightly scared.

"It means," says the guide with a smile, "that the designer of this obelisk thinks it has a voice. It can speak loud, he says. It can talk to us—sort of. What do you think it is saying?" he asks the group.

"Remember," says someone.

"Glory," says another.

"Life."

"Death."

"Pride."

"You're all correct," says the guide. "Frankly, it means what you want it to. The point is it makes you think. At the end of the day, this

---

* The design competition was launched in 1823 by the Bunker Hill Monument Association. The competition attracted fifty entries. Two included obelisks, one by an architect named Robert Mills and one by Greenough. Mills's obelisk (some consider it more of a column) was more elaborate than Greenough's, with inscriptions, decorations, and a viewing platform surrounding the base. The obelisk design that was chosen was closer to Greenough's simpler vision. The actual commission to construct the obelisk went to the noted architect and builder Solomon Willard, who made further tweaks to the design. For a bit more information on the Bunker Hill Monument, see the Afterword.

obelisk has been the source of great inspiration ever since it was dedicated in 1843."

The child, however, is not showing the slightest sign of being so inspired (what three-year-old would be?) and is becoming even more vocal in her plea to go home. But then the guide says something that gets her attention.

"You can walk up inside it," he says.

"Let's do it!" exclaims the child. "*Pleeeeease!*"

The father looks at the plaque outside the entrance to the obelisk. It is 221 feet high, with 294 steps up and 294 steps down, in what is sure to feel like a sauna bath. But he decides to do it, because he wants to get the little girl interested in history any way he can. So they enter the base of the monument and start climbing.

"Put me on your shoulders, Daddy!" exclaims the child, who has gotten predictably tired after about ten steps. The father does so.

Up and up the spiral staircase they go. Several times he stops to catch his breath and says they need to turn around and go down, something the mother has long since done. But after a brief rest, up they go again. Finally they reach the top; the father is gasping for breath, a river of sweat pouring down his face. And then a quick view, and it's back down.

At the bottom he says to his wife in a voice barely above a whisper:

"Let's get out of here. I never want to see one of these things again. I feel like I'm going to die."

And so ends the memory of that day. But there is an aftermath. The father does not die (he never thought he would; it was just a figure of speech). He's young and healthy, his whole life lying ahead of him.

And indeed life turns out to be long and, for the most part, very good. Interesting career options present themselves, including transfers to new cities at home and abroad. The little girl marries, has a child of her own, and successfully pursues a career in academia in California. The mother's nursing career is put on hold as three more daughters are born. They all graduate from college, fall in love, scatter widely, and begin their careers too. They all become fine young women, just as their older sister has. Time passes.

It does for the obelisk too. Its surroundings retain their quaint historic look, but new people move in. Real estate prices soar; the neighborhood is a "hot" market. Most striking is the new cable-stayed bridge that is built nearby. It is a pretty spectacular structure, with suspension cables fastened onto two giant obelisk-like structures on both ends, clearly designed to echo the Bunker Hill Monument across the way. Depending on your angle of vision, the three obelisks form a dramatic entryway into the city from the north. And there is a message here too, because the bridge is named after a noted civil rights and interfaith advocate. The bridge is called the Leonard P. Zakim Bunker Hill Memorial Bridge, thereby linking the historic obelisk to modern issues that were not in the public consciousness at the time it was erected nearly two hundred years previously. Perhaps a new voice for the monument is emerging, one of empathy, compassion, collaboration.

For the family, every day seems to have something to be excited about—or worried about. It's a hectic life with no time to stop and take stock and look back. The years and decades fly by, and in all that time, the father never once gives even a passing thought as to whether obelisks have a voice. In fact, he never thinks about them at all.

Until one day, he suddenly does.

THE EVOLVING CONTEXT OF AN OBELISK

The Bunker Hill Monument in 1848

The obelisks of the nearby Leonard P. Zakim Bunker Hill Memorial Bridge

The view from the base of the monument today

PART I

THE EVOLUTION OF AN IDEA

In which the sometimes-murky thought process that leads a man of complete leisure to embark on a quixotic journey is explained

Background: Egyptian Geography

ASWAN. City in southern (i.e., Upper) Egypt. All twenty-six Egyptian obelisks were quarried here. Capital of the ancient land of Nubia. Elephantine Island and the Philae Island temple complex are both parts of Aswan. Also the site of the massive Aswan Dam built in 1956. Population today: 380,000.

LUXOR. City in Upper Egypt. It was the capital of Pharaonic Egypt in the glory days of the Middle and New Kingdoms. It was known by its ancient Egyptian name of Waset in that era, and then was later

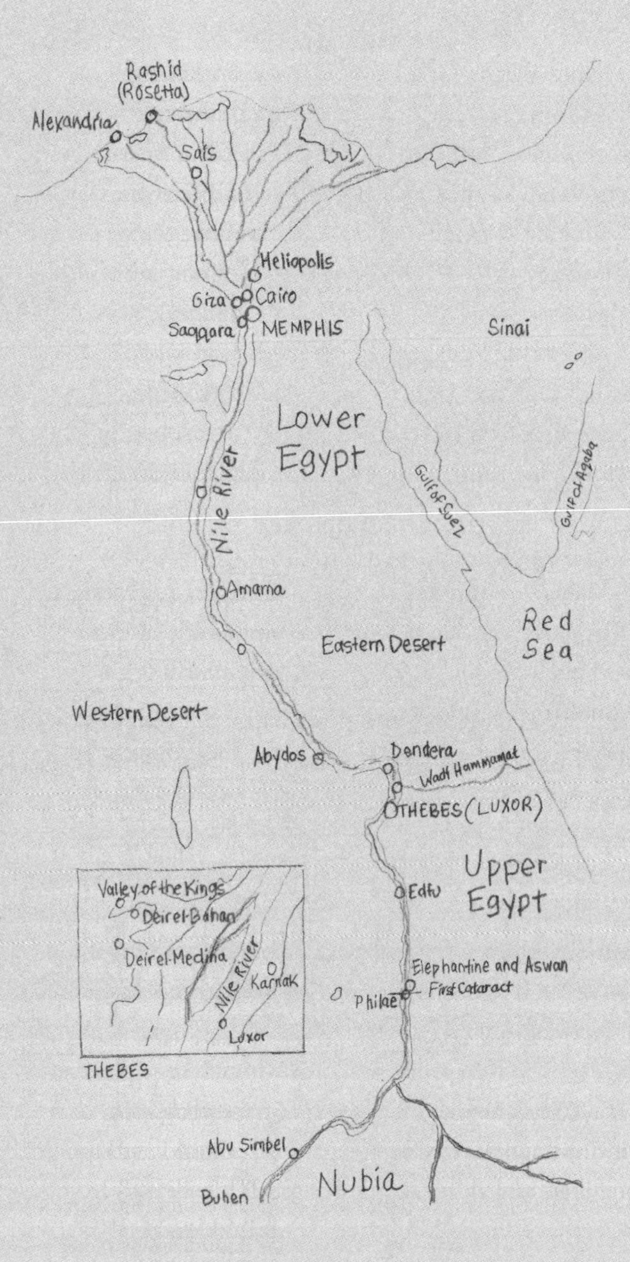

Map of Egypt: Key Obelisk Geography

called Thebes by the Greeks. It is the site of the famous Temple of Karnak and Luxor Temple on the east bank of the Nile. Across the river on the west bank are the tombs known as the Valley of the Kings and Valley of the Queens. Today Luxor has four obelisks: three at the Temple of Karnak and one at Luxor Temple. Today's population is 275,000.

CAIRO. Capital of Egypt. Home to many museums and the Pyramids at Giza and the large sphinx there. The city has three obelisks, all of which have been re-erected there since 1984. Population of the city today: twelve million. Population of the total metropolitan area: twenty million (estimated), which includes neighboring Giza.

ALEXANDRIA. Founded by Alexander the Great in 332 BCE. Chief city of Egypt during the Roman Empire. Sits on the Mediterranean coast near the Nile Delta. Many obelisks that have left Egypt stood here at one time. None do today. Today's population: five million, making it the largest city in the entire Mediterranean.

TANIS (SAN AL-HAGAR IN ARABIC). Major city in Ancient Egypt, now an archaeological site about one hundred miles northeast of modern Cairo. Many obelisks dating to Ramesses II have been found here, some probably having been moved from his capital city of Pi-Ramesses. All obelisks found here have been moved to new locations either within Egypt or abroad.

HELIOPOLIS. Its name means "city of the sun." Once a great city of Egypt, it was the original site of many obelisks. Located in what is now a northeastern suburb of Cairo, it is in complete ruins today.

NILE. Flows south to north, which is why southern Egypt is called Upper Egypt and the north, Lower Egypt. Twenty-five of the twenty-six obelisks were floated on the river from their Aswan quarry to get to their intended destinations. The only one that did not is the Unfinished Obelisk, which still lies embedded in its Aswan quarry.

Chapter 1

ASWAN, EGYPT—DECADES LATER

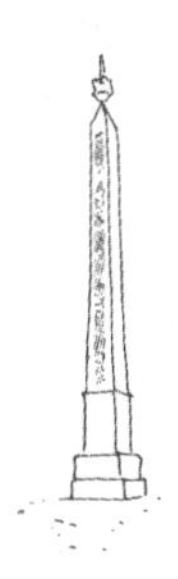

I was sitting on the veranda of the Old Cataract Hotel in Aswan, daydreaming. I am tempted to say "ruminating" or "meditating." But that implies a level of mental focus that I had not reached. I was fatigued, and very pleasantly so, content to look down lazily on the panorama beneath me, letting my mind wander randomly from one half-formed thought to another.

In front of me lay the hotel's swimming pool, a deep azure, surrounded by a well-manicured garden filled with a palette of brightly colored flowers. I'd strolled down there earlier and could recall their exotic aroma. I think I'd seen bougainvillea of some sort. A few of the hotel guests were sitting in lounge chairs poolside, sipping cool drinks in the intense April heat, reading or chatting, or napping. On my lap was a tour book of Egypt that I was occasionally glancing at, idly filling in the blanks on some of the sights we'd seen that day.

I was content and feeling vaguely philosophical, with a touch of self-pity, which is always a surprisingly pleasant sensation, particularly when you have nothing in your life deserving of pity. Here I was staying at one of the best hotels I'd ever stayed at and traveling with two of my favorite people—my good friend and former work colleague Qaisar Shareef—a true citizen of the world, having lived in Karachi, Kyiv, Ankara, and other places before settling down outside of Washington DC—and my LA-based son-in-law, Dana Snyder, a rock star and cult figure in the world of voice animation, and the funniest human being I know. We'd seen some fantastic sights of antiquity that day, and here I was alone, sipping on a Laphroaig, surveying the scene, the Nile not quite visible from the veranda but still a near presence that you could feel. A sense of the passage of time and the evolution of mankind was in the air. As I sat there looking down at the people beneath me, I thought of Orson Welles in *The Third Man*, sitting atop the Ferris wheel in postwar Vienna, looking down at the people below, famously explaining to Joseph Cotton the difference between the ambitious, cutthroat Florentines (who had given the world the Renaissance) and the peaceful, unassuming Swiss (whose gift to mankind was the cuckoo clock).[1]

When it came to worldly success, I was, I thought, much more like the Swiss than the Florentines, my achievements more of the cuckoo clock variety than anything of major importance. Which was fine. I'd led the life I had wanted to, and probably all I was capable of, at least from a business standpoint. But still, there are those moments that beg for an occasional wider perspective, not formally re-evaluating one's life because I was not consciously doing that. But if you spend a whole day immersed in such immense antiquity as can be found in Aswan, you can't help but have a stray, if undeveloped, thought of your place in the universe.

And my place was now abundantly clear. Having retired from a long career with a large international corporation that had allowed me to travel the world, I'd subsequently had a good run as a management consultant. I'd had a steady stream of clients, but now the last one of any consequence said they no longer required my services, and I no longer had anyone else clamoring for my brilliant insights. All of this was fine, actually, since I'd grown bored with working on the same old business issues. The only even marginal effort I'd made to get another assignment was to spend ten minutes in a half-hearted attempt to spiff up my LinkedIn home page. Under "Profile," I'd described myself as a "seasoned veteran," a "mature leader," and a "pro with a long track record." I was hoping to present myself as a trusted advisor with the wisdom of Solomon; instead I'd conjured up an image of a gray-bearded, stoop-shouldered Methuselah whose next consulting gig would be in that Big Board Room in the Sky. Under "Skills," I dusted off a litany of buzzwords I'd long disdained. I was a builder of "ecosystems"; I could break through "paradigms"; I possessed insights that were "value added"; blah blah blah. It was all pretty cringeworthy.

"Is that all I am after all these years?" I thought. "A collection of tired cliches?" In my pursuit to "build my personal brand" (the most obnoxiously-pretentious-but-now-considered-absolutely-essential-practice in the business world today), I had positioned myself not as a sleek new Lamborghini but as a lumbering '59 Ford Edsel with tail fins.

Proclaiming to myself that I was acting out of some ill-defined noble principle, I deleted every word I had written. The LinkedIn world would have to wait for my new profile until I'd thought about this some more. It awaits it still.

At any rate, I was now a man of complete leisure, free to pursue whatever entertainments my understanding wife, Eileen, would allow me to pursue, and with a backlog of Chase Sapphire reserve points that would allow me to stay at places like the Old Cataract Hotel without depleting whatever financial legacy we could leave our four daughters. I was a guy luckier than I had any right to be. But still I was wallowing in a bit of self-pity because—oh, woe is me—I was now an irrelevant, unwanted speck in the universe, just like the nameless, faceless mass of humanity that had preceded me in Aswan for many thousands of years.

Having no one seeking my services was more of an ego problem than a real one. But having nothing to do on a daily basis was infinitely more worrisome. The days would grow tedious without some routine or central purpose, an eventuality that would occur as soon as the following week upon my return from Egypt. I could see myself slipping down the rabbit hole of lying in bed till midmorning, reading on my iPhone nasty reader comments to online news and sports stories from other bored, supine irascibles of a certain age, and responding in kind. I fully realize this was what my daughters might derisively call a first-world problem. But frankly, it was the only problem I felt capable of addressing at that moment.

I got up to walk to the bar and order another Laphroaig, admiring the hotel as I did. To me, it was something right out of the old British Empire, the kind of place you'd expect to see in an old David Niven or Douglas Fairbanks Jr. movie set in the Victorian era. I recalled that one of the most famous Brits ever to have stayed here was Agatha Christie; she had lived in the hotel for several months with her husband, who was an archaeologist and involved with a project in Aswan. She had written one of her better novels here, *Death on the Nile*, a copy of which I was carrying with me. I'm not embarrassed to say I like Agatha Christie, and her having stayed here was one of the reasons I had lobbied for our threesome to stay in this hotel. I'd become something of an Agatha stalker, having once stayed at the Pera Palace Hotel in Istanbul, where she wrote *Murder on the Orient Express*.

As I resumed my seat on the veranda, drink in hand, I remembered something a slightly older colleague of mine had said:

"Fun with a purpose. That's the life to live when you reach a certain point."

It struck me that Agatha had led that kind of life by traveling to interesting places (fun) and writing mysteries in some of those settings (purpose). Maybe it all wasn't fun to her—who knows? But from the outside, it seems it could well have been. Maybe I could find some activity and purpose like that, a central organizing principle or routine that I'd enjoy that could also bring a modicum of purpose to my life (it didn't need to be much).

My mind began drifting back to how we had spent our day. Aswan is a city in a region known as Nubia, the name referring to an ancient kingdom whose northern half is in Egypt and the southern in Sudan. Nubia had interested me because in Boston, where I live, a town square in an African American neighborhood which had been named after a Colonial slaveholder had recently changed its name to Nubian Square, a name with which I was not familiar. Nubians are their own distinct ethnicity, with a very long and proud history. The town is located on the first cataract of the Nile (a cataract being a shallow part of the river, usually with islets and rocks around which the water rapidly flows). The Nile has six such cataracts, and this first one, the northernmost of the six, had given its name to our nearby hotel. Many consider it to be the most beautiful part of the entire Egyptian part of the Nile. The other five cataracts are further south, in Sudan, a place I would have loved to visit but was off-limits then because of ongoing political unrest.

We'd taken a felucca boat ride that afternoon on this part of the Nile, which has been greatly widened since Egyptian president Gamal Abdel Nasser built the huge Aswan Dam in 1956. These sailboats really move along; their three-man crews are expert wind-tackers. We had been greatly amused by the Nubian boys on paddleboards who had approached our felucca, hands out, begging for money. The practice of asking for baksheesh is widespread in Egypt, with some of the more aggressive types almost angrily demanding it. Baksheesh lies somewhere between an annoyance and local color, but we had no problem giving these boys a little something as a reward for their efforts.

The felucca crews are also skilled at docking their boats, which means approaching a dock clustered with other feluccas and ramming their way through like fullbacks plowing through the line of scrimmage, shedding one tackle after another, until they bump into the dock. If the felucca had had seat belts, we'd have worn them. As it was, the only protection we had were the rubber tires that had been haphazardly fastened around the entire perimeter of every boat to absorb the thrust of the ramming—a kind of ancient airbag.

Skimming across the water, we had marveled at how a huge lake had been formed by the dam, resulting in the flooding of the island of Philae. Astonishingly, there originally were no plans to try to save the ancient temple complex and other historical artifacts located on the island. They were to be submerged forever in the new lake. But a Frenchwoman named Christiane Desroches Noblecourt, an Egyptologist at the Louvre, spearheaded the drive to save the artifacts and, most importantly, to dismantle the entire Philae Temple complex, including the famous Temple of Isis, and relocate it. The story of this woman, who had been a founding member of the French Resistance movement in World War II, is engagingly told in Lynne Olson's fine book *Empress of the Nile*. In the end, her efforts, which turned into a major worldwide project involving Jackie Kennedy and others, were successful, and the temple now sits safely on nearby Agilkia Island.

But the thing that made the greatest impression on me that day had nothing to do with the river, feluccas, or relocated temples. It was a visit to the granite quarry where the stone for all of the obelisks throughout Egypt and the world had been mined, sculpted, and carved. In the steaming heat, we'd traveled inland to the quarry, where we were able to see a remarkable sight: the largest obelisk ever created at over 137 feet in length and a full one-third bigger than any other

Egyptian obelisk, which, nevertheless, had never been fully dug out of the quarry bedrock. It had cracked before it had ever been lifted out of the rock, and there it lies to this very day, fully formed on three sides, with the fourth side still embedded in the quarry bedrock. The final step of freeing the obelisk would have involved thousands of workers pounding by hand—literally for years—dolerite subvolcanic rocks around the edges of the embedded obelisk until it was separated from the quarry and ready to be moved to the river, floated to its destination, and erected there. But because of the crack, the final step had never been taken.

The logistics of obelisk creation and shipment are open to debate and are addressed in a number of books; I will not attempt to add any further technical commentary. The point is that this so-called Unfinished Obelisk, lying stillborn in its quarry womb, had left an impression on me. Further, I'd seen a sign in English by the quarry stating that there are twenty-six Egyptian obelisks in the world today—eleven still in Egypt, fifteen now outside.* From this remote spot, all those obelisks scattered all over the world had originated with this unfinished one still waiting to be born in Aswan. This cracked shaft created a connection between the distant past and the present.

I began leafing through the tour book in my lap and found a few pages on obelisks. According to the book, it is believed that these structures are deeply spiritual and are a symbolic depiction of the rays of the sun that emanate from Ra, the mighty sun god. They were typically placed by various pharaohs, usually in pairs, in front of temples as a way to connect themselves to Ra and eternal life. The ancients believed in eternal life, at least for the pharaohs, if not for anyone else. It was good to be the king.

* Actually, the sign by the quarry omits the obelisk in Urbino, Italy, for some reason. When I later discovered this error, I built it into my plans.

Other than what I had read in this tour book and learned touring the quarry, I knew nothing about obelisks and had never thought about them. As I thought about it now in the growing dusk, with the help of another Scotch, it struck me that obelisks were mysterious—a still not entirely understood product built with a spiritual intent to satisfy ambitions for eternal life by bored and probably scared powerful men. Subsequently they were globally distributed through complicated logistics (sometimes with, sometimes without the full consent of Egyptian authorities, but that's another matter altogether). And with newer versions like the Washington Monument now in centers of world power, the obelisk has a distinct and familiar presence and relevance to the modern world. It is maybe the most dramatic example of connectivity between the ancient mind and our own. This subject invited more of my attention.

Eventually my two companions appeared on the veranda ready for dinner, and—as when the man from Porlock knocked on Coleridge's door and interrupted his dreams of Xanadu and Kubla Khan—the spell was broken.*

But, as it turned out, only temporarily.

---

* The English poet Samuel Taylor Coleridge says that while he was writing the poem "Kubla Khan" (1797) in his home in Devon in a dreamlike state (some say it was opium induced), he was suddenly interrupted by a knock on his door from a person from the neighboring town of Porlock. Consequently, he was shaken out of his trance and lost his inspiration, and the poem remains unfinished at fifty-four lines. The "man from Porlock" has become sort of a symbol of inspiration lost because of a sudden interruption.

Aerial view of people walking on the Unfinished Obelisk
in the Aswan granite quarry

Chapter 2

JOURNEY THROUGH EGYPT

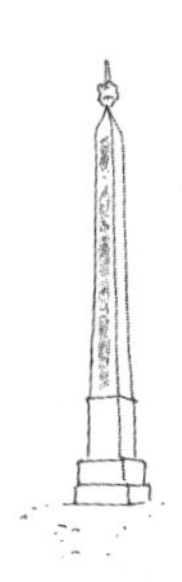

We spent the next week charging through Egypt. Our movement went from south to north, starting from Aswan, not far from Sudan, then on to Luxor, then to Alexandria on the Mediterranean, and doubling back to finish at Cairo. We generally followed the course of the Nile, usually by car, never deviating more than a few miles to the east or west of it, for everything we wanted to see was on the river. Desolation is on either side—the vast Sahara stretching thousands of miles to the west, the desert until the Red Sea on the east.

There are many words to describe travel. Maybe the most common one is *trip*. For me, *trip* implies a pleasant, commonplace activity, a vacation, the elements of which can adequately be communicated in the standard tour book or blog. Most of my travels have been trips. A word that is rarely used to describe travel is *journey*. *Journey* implies movement, adventure, reaching an objective with a chance for self-reflection. I vastly prefer this word. I have traveled a lot, and I have been on many trips. But I have only been on a few journeys.

One was traveling a segment of the Silk Road in Uzbekistan with my daughter Michelle. Samarkand, Bukhara, Khiva! It was the route of the ancient caravans, and I felt myself walking in the footsteps of Marco Polo on his way to China. Another was driving from the ruins of Troy in Turkey across easternmost Greece to what little is left of the town of Ismaros. This remote location on the Aegean, only thirty miles south of the Bulgarian border, is the site of Ulysses' first windswept stop as he attempts to return home after the Trojan War.

In the cliffs of this area, then known as Thrace, Homer tells us Ulysses fought a tribe called the Cicones—an uncommon name, too close to my own for me not to believe that I am somehow their direct descendant, and therefore compelling me to follow Ulysses' route (alas, by land in a Hertz rented car and not on a ship over the wine-dark sea). To the bemusement and often boredom of family members, I have consistently referred to this as my voyage to our ancestral homeland.

Years ago I visited the Greek town of Olympia and on a whim asked an artisan there to depict the scene in Homer's *The Odyssey* where Odysseus clashes with the Thracian tribe, the Cicones. It now hangs proudly in my home office. The quote in the bottom left is from Book 9, lines 44-45.

Still another was walking a segment of the Camino de Santiago de Compostela in Spain. On the Camino one is not a tourist, but rather a pilgrim, with a goal beyond simple sightseeing, striving to attain some often undefinable personal objective. The Camino pilgrim feels connected not only to fellow pilgrims he meets along the way, but also to those who have made this journey before in the distant past, going back to medieval times. A journey involves more thinking than a trip does. A trip is sightseeing. A journey has an underlying hypnotic process.

For me, our time in Egypt began as a trip. By the end of the week, it had become a journey—and along the world's oldest watery byway to boot: the Nile. And little did Qaisar and Dana realize that they were not my only companions on this journey. Several other individuals had now joined me. There was Ulysses, making his way back home from Troy to Ithaca. Also by my side was Herodotus of Halicarnassus, the fifth-century BCE Greek called "the father of history," who wandered the world and devoted the longest section in his *Histories* to a journey through Egypt.[1] I also had a new fellow traveler I had only recently met: Ibn Battuta, the thirteenth-century explorer from Tangier, often called "the Islamic Marco Polo," who had written of the Egypt of the Mameluke era as a part of his undertaking the ultimate Muslim journey, the Haj. I had first heard of him in Dubai at, of all places, a huge retail space called the Ibn Battuta Mall, where storyboards are scattered throughout describing his travels. What a way to shop. And closer to home, I had with me fellow Midwesterner-by-birth Mark Twain and his irreverent fellow Americans traveling with him as *The Innocents Abroad*.[2]

These had all made journeys, not trips, to Egypt. They were storytellers above all, capturing the essence of the place with a combination of vivid description, philosophical musings, and impressions, sometimes with a touch of humor. All were my kindred spirits, whether they liked it or not. The stories of their experiences ended up being my best guides to this land, and not anything I found in Frommer's, Lonely Planet, or on Tripadvisor.

LUXOR

There are a couple of different ways to traverse the 140 miles from Aswan to Luxor. One is by water, on a leisurely Nile boat cruise. The other is by land, either by train or car. Since our time was limited, we chose land, and when we heard that train service was "unreliable," we hired a car and driver. By car there are two possible roads to take. One is the relatively new so-called national highway, which apparently is a modern freeway where the trip takes two hours. I say "apparently" because we never saw an inch of this road. Instead we took an almost entirely unmaintained series of local roads that takes five hours. I never understood why we didn't take the national road. I asked several people and got different answers, the most ominous of which was that the national road is unsafe.

It was a good news/bad news situation. The good news: the local road did provide us some local color as we passed through a string of rural communities, where we saw white-robed locals herding sheep or hauling vegetables in vehicles that looked to be from the distant past. The bad news: the road had a seventy-five-mile stretch where speed bumps had been created every two or three hundred yards. This resulted in continual bone-rattling stops and starts, producing a sensation similar to that of our felucca ramming into the docks, only this time it was every sixty seconds over a three-hour period.

Moreover, on that local road, I saw something I hope I'll never see again. Although the sun had gone down for the last two hours of the drive, none of the vehicles put on headlights. You'd look out onto the road ahead and see nothing, until suddenly a car, truck, or motorbike would appear. Sometimes the approaching vehicle would flash on their lights as we got within a few yards. More often, they turned no lights on at all. It was the same with our driver. He drove with no headlights in the pitch dark as if he were playing chicken with approaching vehicles. In sheer terror, I finally asked him—and later asked other drivers—why no one used headlights. I got puzzled looks, as if I were asking a dumb question. Someone told me that it was thought that putting headlights on drains the battery. But others said it was just common practice. Between the speed bumps and the lack of headlights, by the time we reached Luxor, I felt as shaken as if I had spent five hours on one of those bone-jarring bumper car rides in the dark at an amusement park.

But the trip was worth all the discomfort, because Luxor is one of the highlights of any trip to Egypt. Called Thebes in its heyday, it was the administrative and religious center of Egypt in its glory days of the Middle and New Kingdom (roughly between 2000 and 1000 BCE). When the Arabs conquered the area in the seventh century CE, they called it Al-Uqsur, which, over time, morphed into Luxor. The Arabic word means "the palaces"—which reflects the great number of royal buildings and spaces that are found there. Even today, Luxor bears all the trappings of Pharaonic wealth and power.

On Luxor's west bank of the Nile, where the sun sets, are the Valley of the Kings and the Valley of the Queens. These are the royal burial grounds where numerous pharaohs, their queens, and other family members were buried over the centuries, a kind of open-air Westminster Abbey in the desert. Some of the tombs are astonishing, with brilliantly colorful paintings covering the walls. These walls, which are up to 3,500 years old, look as if they had been painted yesterday, for the dry heat has kept the color from fading. Among many others, this is where the celebrated tomb of King Tutankhamen (King Tut) is located. On the east bank, where the sun rises, are the buildings designed to reflect both the temporal and eternal power of the pharaohs. The most famous is the Temple of Karnak. Karnak is said to be the largest temple in the world, with numerous pharaohs having contributed to its continual expansion over the course of many centuries. So large is it that it almost has a feeling of being a city unto itself.

Much has been written about the tombs and temples of Luxor, and there is no reason to repeat it here. I have already forgotten much of what I have read, along with the tongue-twisting names of most of the obscure pharaohs and queens that lived there. Instead, my time in Luxor further developed the half-formed thoughts of my Scotch-induced reverie on the veranda at the Old Cataract Hotel—a connectivity between the distant past and the present, between the temporal and the eternal. Three individuals had shown me the way.

The first was Ramesses II. Egypt had 170 pharaohs over a 3,100-year span. Ramesses II is widely considered to be the mightiest of the lot.* He presided over great military victories and massive construction projects that are still in evidence today.

But Ramesses did not leave an impression on me because of his awesome power and eternal acclaim. On the contrary, what struck me most was his near anonymity today. It is that which is his greatest legacy, at least to me. For he was the inspiration for Percy Bysshe Shelley's great poem "Ozymandias," which is the name by which the Greeks knew Ramesses.

In 1818, one of the two busts of Ozymandias that were to be found in the funeral chamber in Luxor (called the Ramesseum) was hustled

* When Upper and Lower Egypt were unified in 3150 BCE, Narmer (believed to be the same person as Menes) became its first ruling monarch and was called "king." The earliest confirmed use of the word "pharaoh" applied to an Egyptian monarch was in a letter to Akhenaten around two thousand years later, in 1350 BCE. Today we use the word pharaoh to refer to all 170 monarchs of Ancient Egypt from 3150 BCE to the last one (Cleopatra and her young son known as Ptolemy XV both died in 30 BCE). The territory was then subsumed into the Roman Empire.

off to the British Museum by the Italian archaeologist/former circus performer/full-time looter Giovanni Belzoni. Its greatly anticipated arrival in London led Shelley to write the famous sonnet:

I met a traveler from an antique land
Who said: "Two vast and trunkless legs of stone
Stand in the desert. Near them, on the sand,
Half sunk, a shattered visage lies, whose frown,
And wrinkled lip, and sneer of cold command,
Tell that its sculptor well those passions read
Which yet survive, stamped on these lifeless things,
The hand that mocked them, and the heart that fed,
And on the pedestal these words appear:
"My name is Ozymandias, King of Kings:
Look upon my works, ye Mighty, and despair!"
Nothing beside remains. Round the decay
Of that colossal wreck, boundless and bare
The lone and level sands stretch far away.

For my money, these are the greatest "fame is fleeting/life is brief" words ever written. And as I stood in that very funeral chamber in Luxor, looking at the other Ozymandias bust still lying haphazardly on the ground, the empty landscape in front stretching seemingly forever, I felt the truth of these words more than ever.

The second person I learned about that day was the mysterious Pharaoh Amenhotep IV. He had ruled in Luxor for eleven years before he suddenly changed his name to Akhenaten and packed up and moved his entire regime to a remote area three hundred miles to the north, where he built a great city that modern scholars call Armana. Why had he done this?

For millennia, Egyptian religion had been polytheistic, with twelve major gods (which the Greeks and Romans basically later adopted under different names). Akhenaten said there was only one god, Aten, the god of the sun disc and the supreme creator of all things. This turned Egypt upside down. When he died, his son King Tutankhamen immediately reversed all his father's decrees, abandoned the new city completely, and began the long process of striking the name of the "heretic pharaoh" from all records. Akhenaten's very existence only became known in the nineteenth century, when the ruins of the lost city of Armana were discovered. Today, he is considered to be the founder of monotheism. Wow.

Both the polytheism that preceded Akhenaten and the notion of the sun disc as the one supreme being that he replaced it with at first struck me as very primitive. Yet might there be another angle to consider? Might we someday think our own religious beliefs are equally so? Many people do already. But might their belief that there is no supreme being of any sort also prove to be primitive in the future? I have read that the advancements in artificial intelligence are making a lot of smart people question the way we think about a deity. What AI involves is an entity (in this case Homo sapiens) creating another type of entity (in this case, AI-driven bots, programs, or platforms) that can "think." There is a growing concern that these programs or platforms, which are ignorant of who created them and why, will ultimately be able to think and act for themselves. In a recent survey of PhDs in philosophy, mathematics, physics, and other sciences, a good percentage of the respondents (it may even be a majority) said that the human species could well be a form of AI created by some great intelligence somewhere that, within its own built-in limitations, can think and act increasingly independently from the creator. Akhenaten had indeed opened a Pandora's box of possibilities for me.

And then there is Hatshepsut, the third pharaoh I had "met" in Luxor that day, and one that can be directly connected to our modern world for a couple of reasons. The first is that this highly successful pharaoh was a woman. She was not only the first great female pharaoh but is also considered the first powerful female leader of an advanced society in world history.* In an attempt to solidify her position in a patriarchal society, she had her face depicted on statues and in paintings in masculine garb with masculine traits, including a beard. When she died, her successor and stepson, Thutmose III, began to remove all references to her gender and to claim her triumphs as his own. So did future pharaohs, to the extent that for thousands of years, it was not known that this mighty leader, who had ruled in times of great prosperity and military success, was a woman. It was only in 1830, after the hieroglyphic writing system had been finally decoded, that it was discovered that in a few inscriptions, Hatshepsut is referred to as "her." Ultimately the full truth came out that this pharaoh was a woman who had been haunted by issues of gender identity in her lifetime and marginalized by the men that had followed her. This alone makes her a modern figure.

Her other link to the contemporary world is a tragic one. We had visited her mortuary temple, a beautiful, colonnaded, pavilion-like series of rooms. It is one of the best sights in Luxor, a jewel of the ancient world. But it was in this idyllic spot, of all places, that the geopolitical

---

* Of Egypt's 170 monarchs over a 3,000-year period, there is debate as to how many women were actually full-fledged ruling pharaohs and not consorts or regents. The consensus seems to range between seven and twenty-one. Sobekneferu (died 1802 BCE) is generally considered to be the first female pharaoh, although she was not nearly as powerful and impactful as Hatshepsut seems to have been a few centuries later. On the world stage, the first great female leader is sometimes thought to be Kubaba, Queen of Sumer in Mesopotamia (circa 2500 BCE). But today she is usually not considered to be a historical figure, more legend and myth than real. Hatshepsut was the real deal.

world of today reared its ugly head. In 1997 Islamic terrorists had surrounded the temple and had murdered fifty-eight foreign tourists. I remembered the massacre well. It had destroyed the Egyptian tourism business for years.

Later in the day, we visited Luxor Temple, with its Avenue of Sphinxes. Outside its doorway is an obelisk that lists to its side. Originally it was one of a pair placed on either side of the temple entrance during the reign of Ramesses II. Its mate was given to the French in 1830 and now stands in Paris. This was the first example I had seen of a site where an obelisk had stood for millennia and was now in another country. It would not be my last.

From there it was a short ride to our last stop of the day: the Temple of Karnak, the second-most-visited site in all of Egypt, only behind the Great Pyramid and Sphinx at Giza. As we strolled through it with our guide, Mustafa, he stopped us before two obelisks. One had been erected by Pharaoh Thutmose I, and the other, only a few yards away, by his daughter Hatshepsut.

"You've been to Aswan and seen the Unfinished Obelisk, right?" Mustafa asked. "It was commissioned by Hatshepsut and was supposed to be floated to Luxor and erected at Karnak too. But it never made it. Instead we have this one. The Unfinished was huge, the biggest obelisk ever. But this one is huge too. It's even a bit taller than her father's next to it. But depending on your angle of vision, it looks shorter. See?"

He led us off a few yards to the side and pointed at the two obelisks. From that perspective, Hatshepsut's did appear to be the shorter of the two.

"I think she wanted to build something bigger than her father's obelisk," continued Mustafa. "The massive unfinished one would have dwarfed everything. Imagine how daring it was for a woman of that time to have even thought that way. This one here is still bigger than her father's, though. But being a woman, I bet she decided to present it so it looked shorter than his and not rankle any feathers. Women needed to be sensitive to these things in those days."

Another guide standing nearby, a young Egyptian woman and colleague of Mustafa, overheard this remark, came up to us, and said:

"Don't kid yourself, Mustafa. Nothing has changed in 3,500 years. Nothing at all." And she smiled and walked away.

Hatshepsut, a woman for our times.

After dinner we returned to Karnak for an evening sound and light show. At one point the obelisk of Hatshepsut was illuminated. Above it was a crescent moon. Surely experiencing something so beautiful was enough for a man of leisure, a self-appointed bon vivant and wannabe flaneur. No deeper meaning was required. The beauty of the scene, the music, the aroma of the night air was an end in itself, right? It didn't need to go beyond that moment. It was, in a word, fun.

But I got more than that out of Luxor. It was there that I felt a relationship between the earliest days of civilized man and our modern world. Egypt was far more than a collection of tombs, temples, and art. It had clear connections to the world of the Greeks and Romans, with both societies having learned much from the older one. That I knew. But what I hadn't fully appreciated was that there could be direct connection between the Pharaonic age and ours—some of it literal, some of it metaphoric.

To this insight I owed my new knowledge of some of the famous personalities with ties to Luxor. I can name dozens of famous Greeks or Romans and tell you how they connect to our modern world. Prior to Luxor, I could not have named one such Egyptian. For me, Old Egypt had been populated by totally unknown people, or caricatures like Yul Brynner's Ramesses in Cecil B. DeMille's sometimes cartoonish *The Ten Commandments*. After Luxor, I could name at least a few individuals who, either through their own actions or the accidents of later history, put into greater context for me some contemporary issues. More importantly they gave voice to the universal issues every society has faced, such as the brevity of life and the nature of a supreme deity. My daydreaming in Aswan had turned into pondering in Luxor. Egypt made you think. This was getting a bit serious.

At any rate, Luxor gave me one final thing that later proved to have personal consequences. It was there that I had seen, majestically upright and in their originally intended settings, my first three obelisks.

ALEXANDRIA

Alexandria is the largest city on the entire Mediterranean coast, and we were surprised that very few flights, and none from Luxor, arrive there. Instead, we had to fly to Cairo and hire a car to drive us the final three hours. Of all the cities in Egypt, this is the one I had most wanted to see. A quote from Orson Welles regarding Vienna comes close to how I feel about Alexandria. Welles said this: "The lover of Vienna lives on borrowed memories, with a bittersweet pang of nostalgia remembering things he never knew. Yes the city of Vienna is as fine a city as there is. But the Vienna that never was is the grandest city ever.[3]

"The analogy is not perfect, because it can be said without any exaggeration that the old city of Alexandria was one of the great cities of the world—maybe in fact "the grandest city ever." But I think I understand what Welles is getting at. We cannot travel back in time to fully experience places that have greatly changed. They can only exist in the mind based on a little bit of research and a lot of imagination.

Alexandria has the same effect on me. It has more layers of history than perhaps any city on earth: the Lighthouse that was one of the seven wonders of the ancient world, the Greek era of Alexander the Great and the most famous library of all time, the Roman era of my namesake Mark Antony, Julius Caesar and Cleopatra, the first and most celebrated center of Christian learning, and the place where the author of the earliest Gospel, my other namesake Mark, was martyred. Then came the Arabs, then the Mamelukes, then the Ottomans, then the French and Napoleon, then the Brits and World War II. But now, almost all traces of its former glory are gone. It is now a bustling city of four million and little visited by tourists, who prefer to concentrate on Pharaonic history.

But to me, they are wrong not to go, because the true greatness of old Alexandria is still there, and it always will be. Its greatness is in its location. With its setting on the sea across from Europe and on the trade routes to the East, it was one of the greatest crossroads of the world. Standing at the top of the fifteenth-century Ottoman fortress called Qaitbay and looking out to sea and at some of the rocks in the distance, one can still feel the presence of the great Lighthouse. Built during the reign of Ptolemy II Philadelphus in around 250 BCE, it stood at the then-astounding height of 338 feet, towering over the harbor until three earthquakes reduced it to an abandoned ruin. Its last stones were used to build the fortress on the site in 1480.

Walking at dusk along the nearly ten-mile harborfront promenade that is often referred to as "the corniche" has a sort of magic to it. One can see where Caesar, Cleopatra, and later Mark Antony had launched their fleets of ships into battles throughout the Mediterranean. It was also in a battle in this port that one of Julius Caesar's ships caught fire; the flames spread to the Great Library, causing irreparable damage and destroying some of its 400,000 priceless scrolls, including original texts of Aristotle, Plato, and Sophocles. One can look up the coast to the east and know the waves still crash on the beach of nearby Rashid, where the Rosetta Stone, created in 196 BCE, was discovered by Napoleon's archaeologists in 1799, thereby igniting two centuries of Egyptomania. And only a few miles to the west, one knows that the wind still howls over the sand at El-Alamein, where Montgomery battled and defeated Rommel in 1942 in a battle Churchill considered to be the turning point of the war.

That night we ate dinner at Le Metropole Hotel, which sits just off the corniche. Inside the elevator we took to get to the rooftop restaurant, there was a poster. It read: "Feel the moment! You are standing at the same place of the Cleopatra Obelisk which she had placed here as a tribute of her love for Mark Antony. It is now located in Central Park, New York, USA. Enjoy this once in a lifetime experience, and don't forget to take pictures. The spirit of their love is still alive."

On the poster was a vintage photo of an obelisk lying on its side on a huge wooden platform surrounded by workers in front of the building that is now Le Metropole. Underneath the photo was the caption that I would remember: "The moment when the Obelisk was being removed to the United States of America in 1879."

For the first time, a direct connection had been made for me between ancient Egypt and the United States, and it had come through an obelisk.

CAIRO

After two days in Alexandria, we drove down to a very different place: Cairo. It is a megacity with an estimated twenty million inhabitants in its metropolitan area. It is a place of extremes: of history, heat, poverty, traffic, vibrancy, sights and sounds—of life. In reading about it, it had sounded like Mumbai, a city I'd been to on business and hadn't particularly cared for. So I had wondered if I'd like Cairo. I did, and then some. It is an exceptional example of the integration of the ancient with the modern. There are a few other cities that do this as well. Rome, Athens, and Istanbul come to mind. But the greater Cairo area is in a league of its own because its antiquity predates those other cities by three thousand years, which is pretty staggering when you think about it.

Our guide rightly insisted that we see a few museums there, because they are the best in the world of their kind. There is the brand new and strikingly designed Grand Egyptian Museum (called GEM), in whose courtyard stands the fabulous so-called hanging obelisk of Ramesses II, recently moved there from the ruins of ancient Tanis a hundred miles to the north for the grand opening. We also saw the Egyptian Museum, which houses the largest number of Egyptian artifacts in the world, including King Tut's golden mask. We then marveled at the artifacts of the New Museum of Egyptian Civilization (or NMEC), which has collections from all eras of Egyptian history from the pharaohs to the present day. Its biggest attraction is the Great Hall of Mummies—eighteen kings and queens in all, all brought here from Luxor.

But like the rest of Egypt, Cairo's greatness is not inside museums but outside their walls, where the past and the present coexist, perhaps collide.

The Great Pyramid and Sphinx in Giza. These monuments sit on a plateau overlooking the massive sprawl of the modern city. Built in the reign of the Pharaoh Cheops around 3300 BCE, the pyramid is weathered and has been damaged, for sure, but it still stands as sturdy as a mountain. Although there are remnants of structures in existence elsewhere that predate it, there is no older perfectly intact building in the world. In *The Innocents Abroad*, Mark Twain hilariously (and a bit irreverently) describes how two locals pulled him up step by step on its exterior to the summit.[4] Climbing up the exterior is no longer permitted, but hiking up through the interior tunnel is, and we did it. The roof of the tunnel is so low that anyone over five feet in height is forced to climb much of the way crouched in a kind of duck walk. It was rather difficult in the intense heat, and to take my mind off my pain, I began singing at the top of my lungs any song I knew that included any reference to Egypt. This included such gems as "You Belong to Me" with its opening line "See the pyramids along the Nile," and several by the '60s group Sam the Sham and the Pharaohs (I'm willing to bet no one had ever sung "Wooly Bully" or "Li'l Red Riding Hood" in that tunnel in 5,200 years).

I barely survived the climb, although I'm sure some of the tourists glaring at me wished that I hadn't. It was my Mark Twain moment.

Khan el-Khalili Bazaar. We drove through massive traffic with car horns honking in a constant cacophony of sound until we were dropped off at one of the entry points of the bazaar. We immediately went back in time a thousand years with its medieval byways, sights, and sounds. You can buy anything in this crowded labyrinth of alleys, from exotic spices to underwear. Dana and Qaisar, being better negotiators than I, bought a couple of things, while I was content to just soak in the atmosphere.

The mosques. They line the streets in many sections of town, and we entered a good number of them. Some are new, modern, and crowded, some very old and humble, with one or two old men bent over in prayer. Best of all is walking these streets during the call to prayer, when the voices of the muezzins echo throughout the city. Some have great historical significance, such as the Al-Rifa'i Mosque, where prominent figures of modern Egypt are buried, including the last king of the country, Farouk, who was forced by Nasser and others to abdicate in 1952 and died in exile in 1965. Also interred here, I was surprised to learn, is Mohammad Reza Pahlavi, the shah of Iran. He was deposed in 1979, forced to live in exile, and finally resided in Cairo for the last year of his life. When we visited this mosque, there was a sizeable number of Iranians lining up to see his grave and pay tribute to a ruler who, unloved at the time, is now appreciated among Iranians who bemoan the current regime.

The Coptic churches. Weave your way on foot through the traffic as best you can, and you find a zone with a cluster of these churches. Enter one, and you are in some of the oldest religious spaces in all of Christianity. This includes the church built on top of the cave where the Holy Family was alleged to have stayed while fleeing the murderous decree of King Herod. The Copts, who make up a surprising 10 to 15 percent of the Egyptian population, claim to have the oldest Christian service in the world and trace their roots all the way back to Mark the Evangelist. Interestingly, the Coptic liturgy of today still includes elements of the ancient Coptic language, which was the language of the Egyptian people until it was replaced by Arabic when the Arabs conquered the country in 641 CE.*

Tahrir Square. If such a sprawling city can be said to have a center, this is it. Modeled after l'Étoile in Paris, it is encircled by a swirling roundabout jammed with cars. Some of the most important events in modern Egypt have taken place here. In 2011 crowds gathered here to protest the government of President Mubarak, and his removal from office soon followed. In 2014 masses turned out to protest President Morsi, a democratically elected president, whose close ties to the radical branch of the Muslim Brotherhood and repressive policies led to a military *coup d'état*, accompanied by the ascension of General el-Sisi as head of state. These events had rocked the Arab world and the world beyond. Our guide, Sharein, a mild-mannered, educated woman, told us how she had peacefully protested here and a Muslim Brotherhood neighbor of hers had shot her in her apartment, shattering her shoulder forever. And in the center of the square is an obelisk. The square was renovated recently, and the el-Sisi government, searching for a nonpartisan way to commemorate those who had died here over the years, moved this monolith, erected in the northern city of Tanis during the reign of Ramesses II, to Tahrir. It anchors the square in the same way as the Arc de Triomphe does l'Étoile. Tens of thousands of Cairenes see this obelisk every day. Nowhere in Cairo, in Egypt, or anywhere

---

* In the Nitrian Desert halfway between Cairo and Alexandria lies an area called Wadi El Natrun. With several active monasteries dating back to the fourth century CE, it is still the center of Coptic monasticism. We detoured there and spent half a day exploring this historically important—and truly beautiful—desert community.

else on earth are more people placed in everyday contact with such an ancient link to their past.

* * *

I had one final surprise the next morning. It was at the ungodly hour of 3:30 a.m. when the shuttle bus left our hotel at the airport to take us to our terminal to get our flights back to the US. As I sat in the shuttle looking out the window, still half asleep, I saw in front of one of the terminals a now familiar sight: an obelisk. I later learned that this obelisk, originally erected in Tanis by Ramesses II, had been moved here in 1984. It was another example of the ancient world meeting the modern. It struck me that I'd bumped into so many obelisks and former obelisk sites on the trip. You'd have thought there were dozens—perhaps hundreds—of obelisks throughout the country. But from my reading, I knew there were only eleven still in Egypt, and during the past week, I had seen a majority of them, whether intentionally or not.

We arrived at our terminal, where I performed my final two tasks in Egypt. The first was to pay baksheesh to a man outside the terminal who grabbed my only piece of luggage from the shuttle and carried it into the airport although I had forcefully told him not to. Then, once in the terminal, a second man did the same, carrying the bag to check-in, and then insisted on his baksheesh too. I was out of money by the time I reached the plane, and so I was glad when, in answer to my tongue-in-cheek question, our flight attendant smiled and assured me that she and her colleagues (including the pilot) would not ask for baksheesh in return for their services.

My journey was over. Or so I thought.

The Obelisk at Tahrir Square—the center of protests that toppled two presidents (Hosni Mubarak in 2011; Mohamed Morsi in 2013)

Chapter 3

THE FLIGHT BACK TO BOSTON

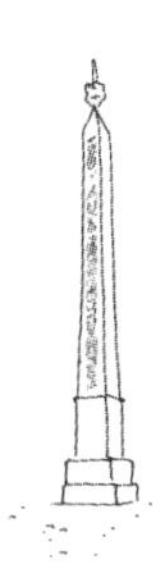

The three of us split up at the airport, with Dana going home to LA, Qaisar to DC, and me to Boston. I had a lot of time to think on the long flight back. A number of things crossed my mind.

First were the Egyptian people. They were friendly without exception. We were greeted with kindness and smiles everywhere we went. Our guides were wonderful, warm, and knowledgeable—eager to please us. I was even OK with the most aggressive baksheesh-ers. Yes, they could be annoying, but I finally concluded that these individuals had very little, and so could I really blame them for begging for a little money from tourists who have so much? They would be happy with ten Egyptian pounds, the equivalent of about twenty-five cents. Big deal.

Second, I'd thoroughly enjoyed the company of Dana and Qaisar. Although we'd had a number of conversations on serious subjects (politics, history, culture), it was the simple, good-natured banter and joking that came to mind first. With none of our wives there, some of it was extremely sophomoric. For example, after our visit to the

Temple of Karnak, we were reminded of the old Johnny Carson routine of "Karnak the Magnificent."[1] It's the one where a turbaned Johnny plays the Swami Karnak and Ed McMahon plays his shill sidekick. Ed gives Karnak an answer, and Karnak guesses the question. It's kind of like a comic version of *Jeopardy!* (a show, by the way, I'd unsuccessfully auditioned for as a destitute college student fifty years previously). Example:

> Ed: The answer is "UCLA."
> Johnny/Karnak (*ripping open an envelope and reading*): What do you see when the smog lifts?
> *(Audience laughs/groans.)*
> Johnny/Karnak: Karnak needs cocktail to get through routine.

Or

> Ed: The answer is "inca-dinca-doo."
> Johnny/Karnak: What do you get on your inca dinca when you leave it on your front lawn over night?
> *(Audience groans.)*
> Johnny/Karnak: Karnak going downhill quick.

That evening in Luxor in our hotel room, Dana played Ed McMahon, and I played Karnak, complete with a makeshift headpiece that defies description. Qaisar captured it all on video on his iPhone.

> Dana: The answer is "Peter of Peter, Paul, and Mary, a lawyer named Clarence, and Ramesses II."
> Me: Name a Yarrow, a Darrow, and a pharaoh.
> *(Qaisar groans.)*

Me: May a diseased yak with intestinal issues dump a present on your front lawn.
Dana: The answer is "you are in denial."
Me: What are you in when your felucca capsizes?
(Qaisar gives a bigger groan.)
Me: Karnak needs new writers.

You had to be there.

The flight progressed with me idly leafing through my notebook. Eventually my mind turned to more practical matters. This trip, which I had eagerly anticipated for so long and had read so much in preparation for, was now over. What would I do now? I pulled out my calendar and reviewed my commitments. Not much on the horizon. Not much at all. I was looking at a lot of totally blank days or mundane tasks, like "get a haircut," or "income tax due," or "go to a Red Sox game." Not very exciting. To my dismay I was back to that evening on the veranda of the Old Cataract Hotel and my pathetic "nobody wants an old-timer" mindset. The first thing I concluded was that I was just going through some normal post-trip depression. I then had the sobering thought that this mood could very well last for—oh, just to throw a time frame out—the rest of my life.

To snap me out of my funk, I went back to looking at my notes and decided I'd begin to write a trip recap for the family. I created an outline, then pulled out my iPhone and started tapping away. After about an hour, I stopped to read what I had written. It was in the format of a chronology—first we did this, then we did that, with a few thoughts sprinkled in. It was quite accurate, with many details. It was also extremely boring. It captured none of the spirit of the trip. In fact, it began to detract from the experience. It was like a photo you take of a beautiful scene. When you look at it afterward, you realize that the moment can never be fully captured, and maybe it is better not to even try. I deleted my recap.

I had already concluded that for me, the week in Egypt hadn't been about seeing sights. It was more an examination of themes, the most important of which was how the ancient world connects to the modern. Does it? How? And is it even important to know if it does? And what is the ancient mind anyway? Is it different than the modern one? Are we truly evolving into some higher order of being? Certainly we know more today. Among other things, we've made dramatic progress in technology and medicine. We can cure illnesses, and we have extreme mobility. Also, despite terrible poverty and economic inequality, many more people today have more opportunity to better their lives than did our forebears. But is that all we mean by attaining a higher order of being? There are so many disturbing things in the modern world, ranging from the hate-fueled culture wars dividing our society to the technological power to do unimaginable evil. You could make the case we hadn't evolved to a higher state at all. Maybe we've even lost something along the way.

In thinking about the trip, the best examples I found of this recurring theme of connectivity of the past to the present were the obelisks. I had seen eight of them in all stages of their lifecycle: conception (the quarry of Aswan), birth (the Unfinished Obelisk there), youth and adulthood (the obelisks in their original surroundings of Karnak and Luxor Temple), death (collapse and desertion at Le Metropole in Alexandria), and finally an unimaginable afterlife (transportation to and resurrection in places like Tahrir Square, Cairo airport, the GEM Museum and, most astounding of all, the Upper East Side of Manhattan). In a very real sense, the Egyptian obelisk was the oldest, most widely distributed human creation on earth and had a unique physical presence in the lives of millions of people every day throughout the world. It was as if obelisks had intentionally positioned themselves far and wide in order to tell the contemporary world something. And I was interested in listening to what they had to say.

But how? What would that look like? Each of these obelisks was different, had its own story, was in its own unique surroundings, and had its own message to be interpreted. To do this right, it would mean seeing every Egyptian obelisk in the world. Did this make sense? Was it possible? I remembered I had copied in my notebook information from a sign I had seen in Aswan that listed the locations of all such obelisks. I looked at the list. Twenty-six, all told. Not a big number. Eleven were still in Egypt, and I'd seen eight on this trip. Fifteen had been taken abroad, and I'd seen some of those already by chance on past trips. So in total I'd seen more than half. Could I visit the others and probably take a second look at some I'd technically already seen but hadn't thought all that much about? I would see them now with new eyes.

I looked at my calendar again. Hmmm. I guessed that I could strategically plan my haircuts to allow more travel. And it would be no loss to skip a Red Sox game or two (they were playing poorly anyhow). True, it would probably mean my film noir classmates would occasionally be denied my insightful comments on Robert Mitchum, Elisha Cook Jr., and Barbara Stanwyck, but they'd muddle through somehow. And on the plus side, more travel would give me yet another reason to cancel a dental appointment and a colonoscopy for the third and fourth times, respectively.

So then and there, I decided to see all twenty-six.

But with what real purpose? Traveling to see all twenty-six would be fun. But it would be even better if there were a purpose, perhaps even some sort of output. Maybe I could prevail on Dana's knowledge of new media and create a series of ten-minute YouTube videos with me in front of each obelisk and offering some thoughts. I was still close enough to the business world to know that this was where the world of communication was heading quickly. Maybe that could be an approach. But it wasn't exactly my style. It started to get into the world of viral marketing, influencers, and online personalities. It was a world I knew a bit about. But it really wasn't me. In fact, a lot of it irritated me.

I was more old-school. I gravitated more to the written word, so maybe my output could be a blog. Or even better, perhaps a series of essays that could appear in the travel section of a local newspaper. Or even more ambitious than that, maybe a booklet, monograph, or good old-fashioned book. I knew finding agents or publishers would be challenging, but I knew some people who had recently gotten their own books published and thought that they could at least steer me in the right direction.

So writing a book which would entail visiting all twenty-six obelisks was what excited me the most. As I thought about it, what particularly intrigued me were the fifteen that are now outside of Egypt. They had traveled the farthest from the quarries of Aswan, and therefore their surroundings had changed the most—often radically so—over time. After seeing them, I would then double back, time permitting, to Egypt and see the three I had missed on the trip I'd just concluded.

But exactly what type of book would this be? Agatha Christie came to mind and how she often used travel as the basis for some of her novels. I liked mysteries, so how about one where the protagonist runs around the world trying to guess which obelisk a crazed terrorist is threatening to blow up? The problem was I had tried to write a mystery before and had given up halfway through, as I had grown weary planting red herrings and MacGuffins and inventing plot turns that had any credibility. I had no desire to try to write a mystery again.

Maybe fiction wasn't for me. Maybe my obelisk book should be nonfiction. I love the travel book genre. As I've said before, I'm not referring to travel guides, but rather to those skilled authors who delve into the history and people along the way and offer thoughts about them. But I demurred. I come up short in many areas, but self-awareness is usually not one of them, and I thought (to paraphrase Lloyd Bentsen's famous jab at Dan Quayle in the 1988 vice presidential debate): "I knew Herodotus. Herodotus was a friend of mine. Mark, you're no Herodotus."

At about this time, I glanced at the flight map on the screen in front of me. We were flying near Greenland. It reminded me of a little book I had read years earlier called *The Ice Museum*, in which the author decides to try to find Thule, the cold kingdom of ice that the Greek explorer Pytheas visited around 330 BCE.[2] His written account is now lost, but through the writing of others, he is believed to be the first person to have traveled into the Arctic Circle and the first to describe the midnight sun. He never identified the exact location of this northern land, and so the land he named Thule has attained mythical status over the years. It was the author's idea to take what seemed to be the most likely candidate locations and travel to each one, investigate, describe their modern surroundings, and come to her own conclusions. These candidates included offbeat places like Greenland, Shetland, the Norwegian archipelago of Svalbard, and Estonia. I loved the concept of the book and thought it provided a basic approach that I'd enjoy.

By the time I had landed in Boston, my mind was made up. I would spend the next year trying at a minimum to visit the obelisks I had not seen, particularly those outside of Egypt. I would then write a short book. I would start each chapter by describing each obelisk and giving some brief background on its history. But many books have been written on this subject by real experts in archaeology and history, and what could a flaneur such as I really add? No, the thrust of my book would be on personal impressions and perhaps adding a bit of cultural context. The picture I would paint of these obelisks would be more like a French impressionistic watercolor than a detailed still life in oil by a Dutch master.

In short, this would be a project without any great pretentions, yet with an innovative take on the subject. It would be the ramblings and reflections of a man of leisure, and not the fulminations of a scholar. It would be a small personal odyssey built around a central organizing principle with an achievable objective: seeing twenty-six Egyptian obelisks, nothing more and nothing less.* On a continuum of undertakings, what I was doing lay somewhere between the self-reflective school teacher who walks the entire Camino de Santiago de Compostela during summer break—making all the stops along the way in order to get the certificate stamp of approval at the end—and the guy who has always dreamt of visiting all thirty major league ballparks and having a hot dog and beer in each.

It would in fact be a journey with a chance to be fun with a purpose. And that's all I wanted.

---

* In addition to these twenty-six obelisks (all of which are quite large and standing outdoors), I later learned that there are a few very small Egyptian obelisks in various museums throughout the world. Most are mere fragments only a few feet tall, hidden in corners of museums that command only a quick look by the observer. Since they are not major monuments standing in prominent outdoor places and, as I frame it, interacting with the external world of today, they fell outside my scope, and I have not included them as part of the odyssey. However, the reader may find some of them of interest, and so I have included them in the Afterword. I have personally seen all of these small museum monuments, except the ones in Durham, England, and Poznan, Poland.

Great journeys, kindred spirits

PART II

THE OBELISKS OF THE EGYPTOMANIA ERA

In which various experiences and encounters lead the man of leisure to begin thinking of "fun with a purpose" in some surprising —and sometimes startling—new ways

Background

With the goal of establishing France as a global empire to rival England, Napoleon invaded Egypt in 1798. In addition to a large number of troops, he brought with him 167 scholars of all types to study Egyptian civilization, which had been neglected for centuries.[1] Although he was defeated militarily, his expedition generated much worldwide interest in—even an obsession with—all things Egyptian and launched what we now call Egyptology. Egyptology became "Egyptomania," which lasted throughout the nineteenth century and resulted in the transfer of four obelisks out of Egypt, two going to England and one each to New York and Paris.

Chapter 4

NEW YORK: SUNDAY IN THE PARK WITH RAMESSES

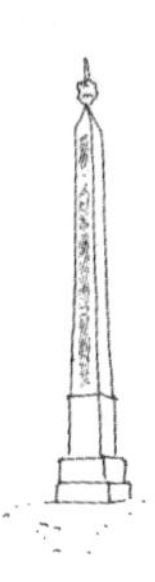

Historical Background

In the thirtieth year of the reign of Thutmose III, in 1450 BCE, two obelisks of red granite quarried in Aswan were erected in the pharaoh's honor in Heliopolis, which is near modern Cairo. They are inscribed in hieroglyphic writing that pays tribute to him. One hundred years later, other inscriptions were added in even more rapturous praise of another pharaoh, the mighty Ramesses II. Thus this obelisk is considered a tribute to two pharaohs. Both obelisks eventually were toppled in invasions and were buried in the sand for over five hundred years.

In around 10 BCE, the Romans discovered them, and Caesar Augustus had the pair moved seventy-five miles north to Alexandria and placed in front of the Caesareum. This was the temple that Cleopatra had built to honor first Julius Caesar and then, after he died, her new lover, Mark Antony. There the obelisks stood for almost 1,900 years, where they became known as Cleopatra's Needles. This is ironic, because she never knew they were there, having committed suicide ten years prior to their arrival at Caesareum.

In 1878 one of the pair was moved to London. The other one ended up in the United States in 1881. Some say it was offered by the Egyptian head of state at the time, the Khedive (the title given to the "viceroy" of Egypt in Ottoman times) Isma'il Pasha, as a token of friendship to the US. Others say the US pressured the Egyptians for the obelisk. The greatest cities of the world—Rome, Paris, London, and Constantinople—all had obelisks now, and some in the US thought that New York, the greatest city of a newly great country, should have one too.

Others were a bit skittish about the prospect. After all, obelisks were the products of pagans, and the tributes inscribed on them to despotic pharaohs flew in the face of the very concept of democracy and the equality of all men. Should America be connecting itself to such impulses? But the temptation to possess such a visibly striking image of history and power was too strong, and the deal went through, with the Pasha finally giving his approval. A ship was specifically designed to transport the massive sixty-nine-foot, two-hundred-ton piece of stone, and it arrived at the docks of Manhattan on Ninety-Sixth Street amid much fanfare. From there, it took a significant effort to transport it to its new home in Central Park, with the construction of special bridges and train tracks that would allow a locomotive to pull it to its location. The three-mile trip took thirty-nine days, some of it in a fierce blizzard, every move chronicled daily by the New York newspapers. These papers had played a key role in convincing the government to pressure Egypt for the monolith, which made the whole enterprise something of a publicity stunt.

The exact location in the park for the monolith had been much debated. Several high-profile places on the periphery near busy streets were considered at first, including Columbus Circle. But the tycoon William Vanderbilt, who had financed some of the costs to transport the monolith, lobbied for Greywacke Knoll, a quiet spot behind the recently opened Metropolitan Museum of Art. He got his wish. Ten thousand people were on hand when it was moved from the horizontal to the vertical position, and they cheered wildly when it achieved its final upright status. It is partially supported by nine-hundred-pound brass replicas of the four huge crabs of stone that were on its original pedestal. Two of the originals are on display in the Met museum.

Buried underneath it are two time capsules. One contains the collected works of Shakespeare, the 1870 census, and a facsimile of the Declaration of Independence. The content of the other capsule was personally placed there by Henry Hurlburt, a journalist for the *New York World* who had tirelessly championed the acquisition of the obelisk. But Hurlburt died soon thereafter and had told no one what he put in there. The Central Park Conservancy, which is the caretaker of the obelisk, says it is not possible to move it to get at the capsule, so what is inside will always remain a mystery.

There is a plaque on the side of the base that translates the stone's hieroglyphs. The plaque was paid for by Hollywood producer Cecil B. DeMille, who grew up near the park and fondly remembered playing near the obelisk. In his movie *The Ten Commandments*, he wrote in a scene of Egyptians raising a monolith. It was his way of paying tribute to the one in Central Park.

Cleopatra's Needle in Central Park is the last obelisk that has ever left Egyptian soil.[1]

Impressions and Context

My obelisk odyssey officially began in New York on a Sunday in May. I'd returned from Egypt three weeks previously, and Eileen and I had driven down to visit her mother on Long Island. It looked like a good opportunity to take the Long Island Railroad into Manhattan and visit the obelisk in Central Park directly behind the Metropolitan Museum of Art on East Eighty-First Street and Fifth Avenue.

As I settled in my seat for the hour-plus ride from the Ronkonkoma station, I decompressed from the weekend so far. Eileen's mother ("Ma" to the whole family) had recently moved into an assisted living facility. She'd hung on as long as she could at her house in Massapequa, but several falls, one of which had resulted in a broken hip and then pneumonia, signaled that now, at the age of ninety-eight, it was time for a change. It had been a bittersweet weekend. We were relieved that she was in a good, safe facility, but sad that she was now moving into a less independent and active stage of life. She had been a great world traveler, having taken numerous trips, from Machu Picchu to Kathmandu. She'd visited all fifty states in a small plane with her late husband, Frank, and their neighbors, the Wilsons. She'd had a great run as a traveler, but that was now in the past. Longevity was one thing, I thought; quality of life was something else. She was doing her best to make the transition. I doubted that I could do it when my time came, which I knew wasn't that far away.

But today there were places to go and an obelisk to see, and so I turned to the task at hand. I opened the leather-bound notebook I now carried with me almost all the time and looked at the first page, where I had written down a reminder of my approach. For each obelisk I would start by giving some facts about its dimensions, logistics, and history. But most of the thrust of my writing would be my impressions and thoughts on their contemporary setting.

And so it was with clarity of purpose and an umbrella in hand that I got out of the train at Grand Central on that wet May morning. It took me thirty minutes to walk up to the Met. Realizing that the obelisk was somewhere behind the museum, I entered the park to look for it there. It had been a rainy day, but by the time I'd arrived, the rain had stopped. The trees and plants were in full bloom, and I found myself in a surprisingly isolated, bucolic spot. The obelisk wasn't immediately visible, and I walked about a bit, searching. I even asked somebody where it was, but they had no idea. "They must be a tourist," I thought. But I walked a bit more, and about two hundred yards behind the museum, there it was, in a leafy, very quiet spot that, despite its proximity to the museum and Fifth Avenue, had very little foot traffic. It seemed off the beaten path. I would determine months later, after my entire odyssey was completed, that of all of the obelisks standing today in urban settings, this one in Central Park is in the most serene spot of all.

As I approached, I saw a small group of maybe six people standing in front of it. They looked to be in their thirties, and I asked them if they were out-of-towners. With a laugh one of them said, "Kind of. We're from Jersey." They had come in just for the day. I asked them if they had come here to see the obelisk, and they said no, they'd come in to see a show and were killing time till then. I asked them what they thought of it, and one of the men said it was OK but not as impressive as another one he had seen. Sensing a kindred spirit, I eagerly asked where that was, and he said, "Las Vegas." He had once been at a trade show held at the Luxor Hotel and Casino. He thought that obelisk was more impressive because it was not only newer and cleaner, but it was positioned dramatically next to the hotel's faux sphinx and pyramid. The three structures dominated that end of the Strip.

This was not the first time I'd heard Americans voice their preference for the architecture of a Vegas resort over the real thing that had inspired it. Years ago I had been in the quaint, medieval town of Bellagio on Lake Como, and two women on a tour out of Philadelphia voiced their disappointment that unlike the Vegas hotel of the same name, the town had no fountain with multicolored water jets coordinated to dance to music. From my point of view, the last thing the town of Bellagio needs is a fountain dancing to the music of Celine Dion.

I then said to the Jersey tourists that I had just been to Alexandria and seen where this obelisk had come from. One of the women asked me where Alexandria was. Was it in Egypt? I'd encountered this kind of thing before; many people just don't have a good sense of—or, I suspect, much interest in—history or place. On a recent flight, Eileen was reading a biography of Charles de Gaulle. She engaged in conversation the young man sitting next to her, who was traveling on business. One thing led to another, and at one point, he looked at her book and asked who De Gaulle was. Presumably he'd have known had we been flying to Paris and landing at Charles de Gaulle airport. But since we were flying to LA, the young man had no such helpful clue.

Hardly anybody majors in history in college anymore, and taking even one course in the subject is not a requirement at many schools for some majors. This is a pity. History is an interesting topic and an important one that sheds light on how we think about the present and the future. But this discussion seems to be over, as staggering student debt and other factors are making the curriculum of most colleges almost entirely focused on getting a job. I guess if I'm honest with myself, knowing where Alexandria is and its history has no bearing on whether a person is a good accountant, nurse, doctor, lawyer, CEO, or tradesman of any sort. And being an unemployed or underemployed expert in history is no fun either. Nonetheless it seems there could be a happy medium here. I believe there once was, and we as a society have started to pay a price for it. What history we do get is often cherry-picked at best, or flat-out untrue at worst, supporting some partisan political or cultural agenda. Not good, and perhaps further evidence that would lead a man of leisure to conclude that we are not moving toward a higher state of being.

* * *

Almost all of the Egyptian obelisks were originally placed in pairs, usually at the entrances of temples or other important buildings. This was not the case, of course, with the obelisk in front of me. It stood alone. But then I turned around to take in a beautiful area with a little pond not far away. As I surveyed my immediate surroundings, I noticed in the distance an extremely tall, thin building. It was easily a mile or more away, but even at this distance, it made a striking impression. The building, although clearly outside the Park (it is on West Fifty-Seventh Street), looked from this angle as if it had sprouted like a giant beanstalk from inside the greenery. Its narrow profile and modern, futuristic design reminded me of some of the enormous buildings I had seen in Dubai, Hong Kong, and Baku, but without the exotic twists and curves that sometimes characterize the buildings of the newest skyscrapers in Asian megacities. I had never seen this building before, its completion occurring only the previous year. It is built on an extremely small lot for a building this tall. In fact, the city of New York loosened its zoning laws to permit it. It is 1,428 feet tall, with an astounding height-to-width ratio of 24:1, making it one of the tallest buildings in the world built on a plot this size. It is often referred to as the "skinny skyscraper," and it's the perfect name. There are two more somewhat similar skinny skyscrapers nearby.

Taking some steps backward, I was able to put the obelisk and these skyscrapers in a single line of sight. It produced a striking panorama that set me thinking. Visually, these skinny skyscrapers were direct descendants of the Egyptian obelisk, which had been the skinny skyscraper of its day. But the new skinny skyscrapers had not been created as symbols of rays of the sun to pay tribute to a god and a ruler. They were created for the practical purposes of commercial development and, in some cases, living spaces. The modern versions reflected the priorities of a pragmatically democratic society, while the original reflected a spiritual mentality that desired to connect directly to eternity. Most would call this progress; some might say something has been lost too. It depended on the angle you took. So although the Central Park Obelisk is no longer paired with its original mate, which is now in London, it has, at least to me, a modern mate on West Fifty-Seventh Street.*

* * *

I was now thinking in pairs, and several more potential mates for this obelisk came to mind as I stood there. One was nearby, almost visible from here: the Temple of Dendur inside the Met. I decided to take a look, so I left the obelisk and walked around the side of the museum toward the museum entrance on Fifth Avenue. I passed the so-called Ancient Playground, a play area for kids which consists of small Egyptian-looking structures. I smiled when I saw one toddler climbing a mini-obelisk in the center. I then entered the museum and saw, next to the information booth in the center of the entryway, a giant statue of Pharaoh Amenemhat II (1919–1885 BCE). The presence of ancient Egypt seemed to be everywhere. I made my way to the giant Egyptology section and approached the perfectly reassembled Temple of Dendur.

---

* This striking structure is sometimes called the Steinway Tower because it is built on top of the building that housed the famous piano company of the same name. Not far from it and also on West Fifty-Seventh Street is another new skinny skyscraper called the Central Park Towers, the tallest primarily residential building in the world. It and the Steinway Tower are the second- and fourth-largest buildings in the Western Hemisphere, respectively. For more details on skinny skyscrapers, see "Exclusive Look Inside the World's Skinniest Skyscraper" by Jessica Cherner and Katherine McLaughlin in the November 9, 2022, issue of *Architectural Digest*.

Mined from the sandstone quarries near Aswan, it was constructed around 10 BCE by the Romans as a way to further solidify the integration of Egypt into the Roman Empire and is dedicated to Egyptian deities and two prominent Nubian brothers. On its sides are various images cut into the sandstone, including Augustus himself wearing Egyptian garb. The temple was given to the United States in appreciation for its role in saving various structures and artifacts from destruction when the Aswan Dam was built in the 1950s and 1960s. Jacqueline Kennedy had spearheaded the American participation in this effort, and in 1963 the temple was disassembled at its site near Aswan and shipped in scores of crates to a new climate-controlled wing of the Met.

The current proximity of the Temple of Dendur to the obelisk is purely coincidental. Yet that is what makes it intriguing to consider them as a tandem. Who could have predicted that two such ancient structures, quarried only a few miles apart in a remote corner of the old Nubian kingdom near Aswan, would by chance end up within a nine-iron of each other in a place that neither the pharaohs of 1350 BCE nor the Romans of 10 BCE had any conception even existed? Taken together, they now represent the location of the most ancient structures anywhere in the New World. The peoples of past millennia would not have been able to comprehend this new setting or the journey their works had taken to get here. Nor can we imagine what this corner of Central Park will look like three thousand years from now. If their future is anything like their past, it is likely neither structure will be here, having been moved elsewhere as trophies for some future civilization we can't imagine.

* * *

The obelisk's quiet setting in the park triggered another unconventional pairing for me, this time a painting: *A Sunday Afternoon* *on the Island of La Grande Jatte.* This work of the French impressionist Georges Seurat was completed at about the same time as the obelisk was moved to New York.* The setting of the painting is a park along the Seine in the mid 1880s, and it depicts average Parisians spending a lazy afternoon strolling, sunbathing, and relaxing. A young girl dances in the background; a couple casually sits on the grass eating lunch; another, dressed more formally, stands observing the scene. Two dogs wander about. Seurat uses the pointillist technique, which gives the scene a hazy look that conveys a feeling of retreat from the everyday, bustling city so close at hand. One can stand by the Central Park obelisk and take in a similar scene—couples holding hands, children playing, a balloon vendor in the background, a small toy boat bobbing on the blue pond in the background. The best place to get the full panorama is to climb up to the top of the nearby Belvedere Castle. Pure Seurat. Of all the twenty-six Egyptian obelisks, this one's location uniquely captures a feeling of escapism.

. . .

My final pairing for the obelisk is with the Statue of Liberty. At first blush they would seem to be an unlikely match. The Statue, unlike the skinny skyscraper and the Temple of Dendur, is nowhere near the

---

* Sometimes called *A Sunday on La Grande Jatte*, this masterpiece was finished in 1886. It is found in the Art Institute of Chicago. It is the inspiration for the 1983 musical *Sunday in the Park with George* (music and lyrics by Stephen Sondheim and book by James Lapine). Also, I learned just recently that I have unknowingly passed the real Ile de la Jatte a number of times. It is a small island in the Seine just west of Paris in the suburb of Neuilly-sur-Seine. A bridge crosses through it that I have walked over numerous times on my way to the office of a company I worked for. Although the Ile still is rather leafy, it also has a number of modern buildings. I never would have recognized the Ile as the setting for Seurat's painting. In fact, the Central Park surroundings by the obelisk resemble the setting of the Seurat painting more than does the Ile de la Grande Jatte today.

obelisk. It is seven miles away in the harbor south of Staten Island. And the two structures bear no physical resemblance, the obelisk being a single stone, the statue a work in metal that was shipped from France to the US in 350 pieces.

But for me, they are different sides of the same coin. They had both been gifts of friendship from a foreign country at a time when the US was just emerging as a world power. And the timing and public discussions anticipating their arrivals in the early 1880s are similar. The statue, its complicated framework and assembly process finally having been devised by Gustave Eiffel after years of struggle, arrived in 1884, just three years after the obelisk. Logistically, both structures had overcome immense odds to get here.

But what makes the pairing interesting is the ideological contrast between them. The obelisk was created by an autocratic ruler who considered himself a godlike figure and whose subjects willingly considered him so. They sacrificed everything for their pharaoh. The structure, pointing upward to the sun, projected otherworldly power. The statue was created for exactly the opposite reason, as a tribute to the equality and freedom of all mankind, her arms outstretched, welcoming the poorest and most downtrodden. The American prime movers who advocated the acquisition of the obelisk were very aware of the fact that the monolith was created by an all-powerful ruler to pay tribute to himself and the gods. All of this contradicts the values and founding principles of the country. But these prime movers felt—or at least convinced themselves—that the projection of power that the obelisk embodies is best represented in a country that is built upon democratic values. In this sense, linking the two structures suggests a dramatic evolution in thinking over the millennia, that power should always be used in the service of liberty for all, especially for the newly arrived to our shores.

* * *

After several hours with the obelisk, it was time to make the walk back to Grand Central. On the way I passed many familiar places which brought back many memories. I had a long history with the city. I had first come here as a teenager with my dad when we made our one and only father-son road trip. I have many fond memories of my father, but that trip is the fondest. I saw a side of him I had never seen—an enthusiastic and fairly sophisticated lover of the big bands and musicals, rather than the quiet, rather introverted steel worker he was back at home in Cleveland.

Years later Eileen and I would marry here, she having been born in Manhattan and raised on Long Island. It was here that we first lived and had our first house after getting married, and where I started with the company that I spent thirty-two years with and that moved me around the world. It's where two of my daughters were born and where the oldest, Christine, had met Dana. As I walked, I passed places with so many family memories, of Broadway shows we had seen, restaurants where we had eaten, unique experiences we had had (such as my ill-fated audition for the TV show *Jeopardy!* when I was a destitute college student looking to make a quick buck).

Nathaniel Hawthorne, in his preface to *The Scarlet Letter*, writes of the benefits of people and families living in different locations over the course of their lifetimes. He says that just as crops can grow unproductive if they remain in the same soil too long, so too must people seek out new "unaccustomed earth" to grow and remain vibrant.[2] I believe this wholeheartedly and have advocated that all family members seek unaccustomed earth. But humans also benefit from having continuity, familiar fixed points that they can turn to. They need a center. New York is one such fixed point for me. In that sense, the city to me is like the obelisks were to the ancient Egyptians—familiar points of reference they could turn to as time passed on.

* * *

So what did the Central Park obelisk say to me? It told me the story of movement, from its creation in a remote quarry and its four-hundred-mile journey down the world's oldest watery highway to a place dedicated to a queen's two lovers, then a three-thousand-mile sea voyage to New York Harbor passing directly over the soon-to-be site of its ideological statue-bookend created in France three thousand years later with its entirely different message, then on to a quiet corner in a beautiful park where an old sandstone friend from its hometown would eventually join it and stand one hundred yards away from it in a museum. Its message was one of a connection to a supreme entity based on a faith that was at once primitive and profound. Its original message involved the subordination of the rights of the common man to its ruler, but it was now in a place where those rights are espoused. It is a testament to the power of context—its original placement meant to elicit awe, its new one offering a peaceful respite for just ordinary folks to relax and kids to play ball or jump rope.

Above all it was telling me a story of the necessity to evolve and change, but, paradoxically, of the human need for continuity. It was a complex, nuanced story best told by a poet who could simplify it. But a man of leisure hasn't the skills to do that. Too bad Shelley isn't still alive.

The Luxor Hotel and Casino on the Las Vegas Strip

The Central Park Obelisk (with the skinny skyscrapers in the background), alongside its Las Vegas alter ego

Chapter 5

PARIS: KEEPING ONE'S HEAD IN HEAVY TRAFFIC

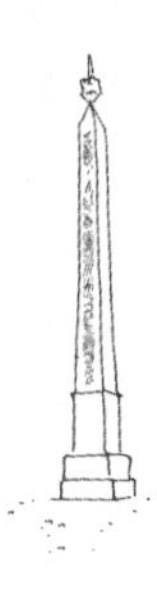

Historical Background

In the reign of Ramesses II, around 1250 BCE, two obelisks of red granite from the quarries in Aswan were shipped by barge a hundred miles down the Nile. They were placed on either side of the main entrance to the Temple of Luxor, which had been built 150 years earlier. There they both stood until the early nineteenth century, when the Ottoman governor Muhammad Ali gifted one to the French. The other one, slightly taller, still stands by the temple in Luxor to this day, listing slightly.

The French had long wanted an obelisk, a desire that became an obsession in the time of Napoleon. As a way to prove to the world that France had now become a global power on par with the British Empire and the Roman Empire before it, the Corsican's fleet of ships, with thousands of troops, sailed into Alexandria in 1798, looking for military conquest. They were also accompanied by 167 scholars eager to study the country's antiquities and hell-bent on bringing some back both as geopolitical trophies and as objects to study further. Napoleon and several of his scholarly entourage had originally wanted to take at least one of the two obelisks, now called Cleopatra's Needles, that stood in front of the Caesareum in Alexandria. But Jean-François Champollion, the most credible of all French Egyptologists because of his breakthrough translation of the Rosetta Stone, insisted on one of the two at Luxor Temple instead, saying it was of more historic interest. And so it was that the Luxor obelisk was moved to Paris and installed in the middle of the Place de la Concorde.[1]

This square is one of the most iconic spaces in all of France, partially because of its very dark history. In the French Revolution of the 1790s, 1,119 people were guillotined there, including Marie Antoinette and Louis XVI. Formerly called Place Louis XV before the revolution, it went through several name changes until it was given its current name in 1823. The thinking was to promote reconciliation between the ruling, bourgeois, and working classes whose hatred for one another had ripped France apart for decades. The obelisk was deemed to be a totally apolitical symbol of historical greatness that, importantly, had no connection to any French faction.

The transfer of the monolith from Luxor to Paris had been very difficult. No major obelisk of this size had been moved out of Egypt for over 1,500 years since one had been moved from Alexandria to Constantinople by the Romans in 357. But through a series of smart engineering workarounds, the obelisk arrived at the square in 1836, never having been split into smaller pieces as others had been in previous movements out of Egypt.

Since the original pedestal was considered too risqué because it included images of four naked baboons with genitalia showing, a new one was created with a rendering in gold of the complex apparatus that was used to lower the obelisk in Luxor and raise it in its new location.

Flanking the obelisk on either side are two fountains, one devoted to the maritime history of France, the other to its rivers. They were the idea of the architect Jacques Hittorff, whom Emperor Louis Philippe had commissioned to redesign the square to commemorate the anniversary of his coronation as emperor. Hittorff got the idea after visiting Rome and seeing the two fountains that flank the obelisk in St. Peter's Square and Bernini's famous Fountain of the Four Rivers in Piazza Navona, which is flanked by its own obelisk, created by the Roman emperor Domitian.

Finally, in other recent news: on June 20, 2023, a striking golden tip in the form of a pyramidion was placed on the top of the obelisk. It had been without a top since it had been brought to Paris from Egypt. Also, the Place de la Concorde was converted into an "urban sports park" for the 2024 Paris Olympics and was the site of several events, including skateboarding and BMX (bicycle motorcross). If the Pharaohs only knew . . .

Impressions and Context

I wanted to see this obelisk on my own terms, which meant, since this was Paris, going into full flaneur mode for the day. I initially thought that buying a loaf of bread at a boulangerie near my hotel would be the most appropriate way to start the day, but decided instead to find some atmospheric little sidewalk cafe on the Left Bank and have a croissant and café au lait. So I headed out of my hotel on a warm, sunny morning in the City of Light, cafe hunting.

I had decided that it would help me look the part of a typical Parisian if I brought along some authentically French reading materials that I could ostentatiously flaunt as I ate (optics are important for a flaneur). My initial thought was to go to a bookshop and buy something like the novel *La Nausée*, by Jean-Paul Sartre. However, I quickly remembered two things: 1) my high school French had never been good enough to understand Sartre, and 2) I never knew what the hell existentialism was anyhow. So instead I stopped at a newsstand and bought the latest editions of *Le Monde* (to show my interest in world affairs) and *L'Équipe* (revealing the sporty side of me that was interested whether Kylian Mbappé would leave Paris Saint-Germain and jump to the English or Spanish League—this is very important information for the Parisian man-about-town). Newspapers in hand, I then spotted a little place called Le Petit Fou-Fou and sat down at an outside table, hoping to hear a recording of Edith Piaf singing "Non, Je Ne Regrette Rien"—or better yet Ella Fitzgerald and "April in Paris"—as café background music.

My experience at Le Petit Fou-Fou did not go according to plan. First, the other patrons of the cafe were not authentic Left Bankers but other tourists like me. The men were wearing Bermuda shorts, and the young man sitting next to me was wearing a New York Yankees baseball cap. Second, my French was not even good enough to read the newspapers (I couldn't tell if Mbappé was coming or going). Then I thought I'd try to speak a little *français*, reasoning that although my French was too primitive to allow me to explore existentialism, it might be good enough for me to order a croissant. So I raised my hand as the waiter passed, intending to say "I would like to order; I am ready ("Je voudrais commander; je suis prêt"). Here's what transpired.

Me: "Garçon."
Waiter *(coming over)*: "Oui, Monsieur?"
Me: "Je voudrais commander. Je suis prêt."
Waiter *(looking puzzled)*: "Comment? (What?)"
Me *(a bit louder)*: "Je suis prêt."
Waiter *(still puzzled)*: "Je ne comprends pas (I don't understand)."

> Me *(frustrated and wondering if this guy is a college student from Kansas City who has taken a summer job in Paris to brush up on his French)*: "Je suis prêt! Je suis prêt! Je suis prêt!"
> Waiter *(irritated and in good English with a French accent)*: "Sir, you say you are a priest. You keep repeating, I am a priest! I am a priest! I am a priest! What do you want me to do?"

I had mispronounced "prêt." The word ends in a soft *t*. In my effort to use what I thought was authentic French pronunciation, I had mimicked the scratchy, slightly guttural sound that I'd heard my French son-in-law use when ending some words. This turned "pret" from meaning "ready" to "pretre," which means "priest."

> Me *(thoroughly deflated)*: "OK, buddy. Gimme a croissant."

I guess if I'd thought quickly enough, I could have played along and said I was asking if there was a discount for clergy members. Instead, I rifled the croissant down, and when the music in the background turned out to be not an Edith Piaf torch song but rather some *American Idol*–like caterwauling, I knew it was high time to leave. So I gathered up my copies of *Le Monde, L'Équipe*, and what was left of my pride, and made my way to Place de la Concorde.

* * *

The Place de la Concorde is at the eastern end of the Champs-Élysées, and the Arc de Triomphe is at the western. Channeling François Truffaut, I made my way by Metro to the Arc and from there began walking the 1.5 miles down the avenue toward the other eastern end. Gene Kelly in *An American in Paris,* Louis Jourdan in *Gigi*, Maurice Chevalier in a dozen movies—every bon vivant worth his salt had made this walk. I had done it before too, but either as a tourist or when staying in the city for work. This was different. Today I was a carefree boulevardier, and the fact that the most famous street in Paris—and maybe the world—is now lined with global retailers (and even a McDonald's) and has a constant flow of Uber Eats bicycles making home deliveries rather than horse-drawn carriages, didn't alter my mood. I know they are rethinking a way to return the Avenue to its glory days, with traffic restrictions and building pathways through gardens. Hopefully the rather everyday commercialism that has gradually taken over the street will be but a brief moment in time. At any rate, I preferred to think of this 1.5-mile stretch as the elegant, historic, and uniquely French *rue* it was (and still is) at heart—the place where young men wearing straw hats strolled with their lovers, where wild celebrations took place in 1944 when the city was liberated from the Nazis, where joyful patriotic parades occur every Bastille Day on July 14, where the pageantry of the final stage of the Tour de France takes place.

I was in a lighthearted mood when I reached the Place de la Concorde, the largest square in Paris. A heavily trafficked roundabout encircles the square. Along with a crowd of tourists, I waited at the crosswalk until the traffic light allowed us to go. In a minute I was face-to-face with the obelisk.

▪ ▪ ▪

Standing at the base of the obelisk, one is afforded several perspectives of the most iconic sights in France, perhaps in all of Europe. The most famous is the view up the Champs-Élysées, past the Petit Palais and Palais-Royal and with the Arc de Triomphe at the end. The modern Arche de la Défense stands beyond that. Together, the axis of these perfectly aligned structures is often called the Voie Triomphale, or the Triumphal Way. Turning in the opposite direction, one sees the gate into the greenery of the Tuileries Garden, which leads into the Louvre. If you look upward, the Eiffel Tower, with its "nouveau industrial" design, appears nearby.

Height is one of the physical characteristics one always thinks of regarding obelisks. In fact, they have been called the world's first skyscrapers. In that light, it is interesting to consider this obelisk and the Eiffel Tower as a pair. When the latter was erected in 1889, it became the tallest building in the world and remained so for forty-one years, until the Chrysler Building in New York was completed in 1930. The structure that the Eiffel Tower supplanted as the tallest in the world?

Drum roll, please: an obelisk, namely the Washington Monument in Washington, DC. It had superseded the Cologne Cathedral in 1884. In modern times the competition to claim the title of world's tallest building has heated up, with new winners popping up every ten or fifteen years in various countries across the globe. But the Egyptians hold the longevity record—and with a pyramid, not an obelisk. The Great Pyramid of Giza was the world's tallest structure for over an astounding 3,700 years (2570 BCE to 1221 CE). It is a "tallest building in the world" record for longevity that probably will never be broken.

But it is the ground on which the obelisk stands that leaves you with the greatest impression, for it was here, between 1792 and 1794, that over one thousand people were guillotined during the French Revolution, including the king and queen, and later some of the leaders of the Revolution itself, including Danton and Robespierre. The French Revolution was a complicated event with various interpretations. But it led to the so-called Reign of Terror, which all can agree is one of history's most powerful examples of idealism run amok, the triumph of demagoguery over reasoned debate. It was political, cultural, and class warfare at its worst, with former allies and even families turning against themselves.

The Revolution soon inspired other French insurrections, with everyday citizens manning the barricades in 1830 and 1848. The Paris Commune of 1871 followed, with more insurrection and death. Indeed, Paris has a history of protests that has carried through to this day, and Place de la Concorde is at the heart of it. For example, in the 1990s, the entire obelisk had been covered in a wrapping that was meant to be a giant condom as a protest against the slow progress in finding a cure for AIDS. And even as I stood there on this May morning, a group of young people wearing the yellow vests that are now symbols of contemporary protest had a booth set up at the base of the obelisk, passing out leaflets of protest and seeking support for their next efforts to paralyze the city. Most of this is nonviolent and actually an example of democracy in action. After all, it is the French who gave the world the rallying cry of "liberty, equality, and fraternity." But it's the dangers of the potential for a mob mentality that give you pause. History teaches us that all it has ever taken is one slick demagogue to convince seemingly rational people to cross the line from rightful protest into a self-righteous mob.

The comparisons and contrasts between the American and French revolutions are obvious. Our Founding Fathers were extremely influenced by the French thinkers of the Enlightenment and were true to that movement's spirit while, ironically, many French revolutionary leaders were not. But one big difference was that the Americans were fighting an external foe, the British. The French were fighting among themselves, which is much more dangerous and much more capable of destroying a powerful country than any external threat. The US had to learn that itself when it tried to rip itself apart in its own Civil War.

Again the obelisks were speaking to me. They almost seemed to be arguing among themselves across the ocean, with me eavesdropping.

The one in the Place de la Concorde was loudly telling a tale of a history that was at once glorious and very disturbing. The one I had recently visited in Central Park was answering with words of peacefulness spoken in a hushed voice. In tone, the one in Paris is much closer to the one in Tahrir Square in Cairo—both symbols of freedom, yes, but also of conflict, with dark undercurrents. At the heart of this darkness is what some scholars say was the single greatest concern of the Founding Fathers of the United States: the potential for just a very few persuasive individuals—maybe even just one demagogue—to emerge and incite a mob to further their personal agenda. George Washington explicitly warned of this. Twenty-two separate framers of the Constitution used the word "demagogue" in speeches at the Constitutional Convention. And Alexander Hamilton wrote in *The Federalist Papers:* "History will teach us that . . . of those men who have overturned the liberties of republics, the greatest number have begun their career by paying an obsequious court to the people; commencing demagogues, and ending tyrants."[2]

It had happened in the Place de la Concorde in Paris in 1793, where an obelisk now stood, and I wondered if it could happen today in Central Park too. I concluded that if it was enough to worry the Founding Fathers—men who had studied deeply the Greeks, Romans, and other civilizations and had seen disturbingly reoccurring patterns—it was probably enough to worry a man of leisure too.*

. . .

* What makes this a tricky discussion is the obvious fact that one person's forked-tongue demagogue is another person's truth-telling, mellifluous orator. What complicates things even more is something that the Founding Fathers never could have foreseen: that the next demagogue might not even be a human being at all but some AI-driven digital creation that spreads lies and misinformation for its own sinister purposes. Good grief! As Bette Davis says in the 1950 movie *All About Eve*: "Fasten your seatbelts, everyone. It's going to be a bumpy night."

I was now entering dangerous mental territory. I had entered the Place de la Concorde as Gene Kelly, clicking his heels, about to meet up with Leslie Caron. I was leaving it as Dickens's Sidney Carton in *A Tale of Two Cities*, standing in a pushcart on his way to a date with Madame Defarge. This is not how it's written up in the "How to Be a Bon Vivant" manual. Nor is the next stop I'd planned: a cemetery. What had I been thinking?

Actually my logic had not been all that outlandish. The Père Lachaise Cemetery is a legitimate tourist attraction, with the graves of many famous French men and women here in beautiful surroundings. What drew me was that this cemetery is considered by some to be the unofficial birthplace of the obelisk as a grave monument. In 1804 Napoleon, because of plague and disease that were rampant in Paris, ordered the creation of a new burial ground on the outskirts of the city for health and sanitation reasons. He commissioned Alexandre-Théodore Brongniart, a well-known architect, to design the space. When Brongniart had traveled to England, he had fallen in love with the well-manicured gardens there and used them as a model for Père Lachaise. He and the artisans who created the tombs were well aware of the Egyptomania that now gripped Paris after Napoleon's well-publicized adventure there, and the obelisk became an intriguing structure to commemorate the dead. It was impressive; it had other worldly connotations; and since it went upward and not sideways, as does the typical mausoleum, it is a space saver. Although Père Lachaise does not have the first obelisk grave in history, it helped to popularize it and was a force behind its spreading to other countries.

Despite its lugubrious connotations, my walk through Père Lachaise Cemetery boosted my spirits. For one thing, I enjoyed seeing the memorials to the many famous people here, such as Proust, Piaf, Molière, and many others. The grave of the lead singer of the Doors, Jim Morrison, still gets flowers from his fans. I'm something of a fan too. Not only do

I like their sound, but I like their name. It's lifted from Aldous Huxley's weird autobiographical book *The Doors of Perception*, which is itself lifted from a line in the even weirder book by William Blake, *The Marriage of Heaven and Hell.* The Doors is a far more impactful name than, say, the old British rock group Gerry and the Pacemakers, which conjures up an image of a heart monitor apparatus.

But the main things for me there in the cemetery were the many obelisks. They were scattered everywhere. I smiled when I saw that the grave marker of the most famous Egyptologist of all, Jean-François Champollion, is an obelisk. And there were a number of others that commemorate groups, such as soldiers who died in a specific war or battle. Such war memorials are now prevalent around the world, and they owe at least a bit of their popularity to this cemetery that pioneered the structure. To me it is yet another example of the global reach of the Egyptian obelisk.

I left the cemetery in good spirits. I was once again a boulevardier. But is it an oxymoron to say I was a more pensive one?

* * *

The next day, it was off to the Gare du Nord to catch the Eurostar train that would travel under the Channel and, in little more than two hours, would drop me off at the St. Pancras station in the heart of my next stop, London.

The Paris obelisk at the Place de la Concorde: a dark past in the City of Light

Chapter 6

LONDON: OF TIME AND THE RIVER

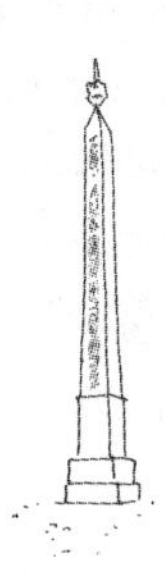

Historical Background

The obelisk in London is one of the two so-called Cleopatra's Needles, its mate now in New York's Central Park. To briefly review some facts:

Both Cleopatra's Needles are monoliths of red granite quarried in Aswan during the reign of Thutmose III in about 1450 BCE. They were subsequently erected in Heliopolis, were then rededicated to Ramesses II one hundred years later, and then moved by Caesar Augustus in around 12 BCE to be placed in front of the Caesareum in Alexandria. Fast forward to 1819, when the Ottoman pasha and de facto ruler of Egypt, Muhammad Ali, seeking to solidify military alliances with the two great world powers, gave one obelisk to England and one to France. France ultimately turned this offer down and successfully lobbied for the rights to one of the obelisks at Luxor Temple, which now stands in the Place de la Concorde in Paris. The Alexandria obelisk that the French rejected was later given to the United States, who moved it to Central Park in 1881.

The other Cleopatra's Needle, still left in Alexandria, had long since toppled over and had lain in the dust for centuries. It was offered to the British in 1819 by Muhammad Ali. The English accepted it, but, due to the high costs to move it, they did not do so and eventually lost interest in it. There the monolith continued to lie, almost forgotten for over fifty years, until 1876, when a midlevel British Army officer named James Alexander saw it and began to drum up support to move it to London. On a trip to Paris, Alexander had seen the obelisk in the Place de la Concorde and thought that England should proudly display one too as a sign of its power. After all, reasoned Alexander, Admiral Nelson had destroyed Napoleon's Egyptian fleet way back in 1800, forcing the French to militarily evacuate Egypt and allowing the British to claim and bring back to England many of the famous antiquities the French had been planning to bring back, including the prized Rosetta Stone. So it was only fitting that the fallen obelisk in Alexandria, to which the English already had rights, should end up in London. Ultimately, Alexander raised the funds, and its transfer to England began.

Of all of the twenty-six obelisks quarried in Aswan, this one endured the most treacherous voyage any of them ever made. A strange-looking cylindrical ship was specifically designed to accommodate the shape of the Needle and enable it to make its watery trip from Alexandria to British soil. This ship, dubbed the *Cleopatra*, had no power of its own and needed to be tugged all the way to England. The *Orca*, the boat doing the tugging, made it safely out of the Mediterranean with the *Cleopatra* in tow. But in the Bay of Biscay, between France and England, they ran into a ferocious storm that sank the *Cleopatra*. In trying to rescue the crew of the *Cleopatra*, six members of the *Orca* died. It was thought that the ship and obelisk had sunk and been lost forever, but remarkably the *Cleopatra*, with the obelisk, was later found floating in the bay by the British steamer *Fitzmaurice* and towed to England.

There ensued a debate as to where the exact placement of the Needle should be. Eventually the decision was made to erect it on the Victoria Embankment, a long and elevated road and river walk along the Thames newly created in 1870 as a part of a modern sewage system and also to alleviate the traffic in the area. It was erected atop the Embankment between Waterloo and Hungerford Bridges. Time capsules were placed underneath it.

In 1878 two faux-bronze sphinxes were created to flank it, as if to stand guard over it. On its pedestal are inscribed the names of the men of the *Orca* who were drowned in the Biscay storm. In 1917 a German air blitz bombed the area, damaging the pedestal and making it the only obelisk ever damaged in modern warfare. The pedestal remains unrepaired to serve as a memorial of the blitz.

In 2015 the famous Egyptian archaeologist Zahi Hawass said that the maintenance of both the Needles, in London and New York, was poor, and if it was not improved, they should be returned to Alexandria. Since then, there has been greater attention to preservation, and these measures remain in place.[1]

Impressions and Context

The Embankment Underground tube station is a familiar one for me. Several of the London walking tours I have taken over the years have passed by it, usually without a word of comment. These tours, with names like "Dickens's London," "Shakespeare's London," "The Beatles Tour," "In the Footsteps of Jack the Ripper," and many others, are always led by articulate, passionate, and often humorous individuals who are sometimes even dressed in period costumes (my favorite is the guide for the Elizabethan tour who dresses as a jester and carries a lute around).[2] Today I was meeting the MI6 tour, which would explore the world of that famous intelligence agency. I wanted to take this tour today as well as head up by train the next day to Bletchley Park, the English country house and estate north of London that had become the principal center of Allied codebreaking during World War II. I thought this would be useful background research for my upcoming trip to see the other Egyptian obelisk in England, which is in Dorset. But more on that later.

I arrived at the tube station early, because the London obelisk is located near it, just a two-minute walk away along the Thames. I had passed this obelisk dozens of times over the years but, frankly, had taken little note of it. It was a classic example of why, although I had seen some of these obelisks before, I needed to see them again now. I wanted to hear what they had to say.

I approached it by way of the very pretty and often overlooked Embankment Park, passing by statues of individuals who are both famous (Robert Burns) and barely remembered (Henry Fawcett).I smiled as I passed the wonderful memorial dedicated to the Imperial Camel Corps. It depicts a soldier sitting jauntily atop a camel, and the pedestal bears the inscription:

> *To the Glorious Immortal Memory of the Officers and NCOs and men of the Imperial Camel Corps, British, Australia, New Zealand, Indian, who fell in action or died of wounds and disease in Egypt, Sinai, and Palestine 1916–1917–1918.*

Troops from this unit fought alongside T. E. Lawrence in 1918 in the so-called Revolt in the Desert. Some undoubtedly saw obelisks in situ as part of the Egyptian Expeditionary Force, making the memorial's placement here quite appropriate, if little-noticed today. The obelisk is very close by and easily seen from this memorial.

As I drew near the monolith, what struck me was its location on the banks of the river. Not one of the other twenty-five obelisks is on the water. This is somewhat surprising, since they are so closely linked to a river. Without the Nile, none of them could ever have been moved from their Aswan quarry. The river had transported all of them, some of them multiple times. But today none save this one are directly on the water. (One other had been on Gezira Island, in the middle of the Nile in Cairo, but it had recently been moved to the new city of El-Alamein in the north to bolster the image of that area for future development. These obelisks got around . . .[*3])

I've always liked rivers. They are useful, they often flow through beautiful landscapes, and many are at the heart of my favorite cities. I have a particular soft spot in my heart for the Thames. England was the first country I had visited outside the US at the remarkably old age of thirty. I had pent-up travel needs, and I had built up huge expectations for that trip. London exceeded all my expectations, and the Thames was a huge part of it. Along its shores I saw places I had visited in my mind's eye many times: the pretty Cotswold towns near its source, near Cirencester; Oxford and the many historical figures who had studied there; Windsor Castle and the monarchy; Runnymede and the Magna Carta; the palaces at Hampton Court and Greenwich; and Canary Wharf and the great shipping hub toward the Thames Estuary, which flowed out to sea with ships carrying cargo. Coming in and going out, they make England the global center of commerce.

And here was the obelisk standing riverside, looking over it all. What might it be thinking about all this? For one thing, I thought it

* This obelisk shows how these monoliths continue to be moved to this very day. This obelisk was erected near the northern city of Tanis during the reign of Ramesses II (1279–1213 BCE) and moved to the Gezira Island, where it was raised in 1960. It stood there for fifty-nine years until it was moved to its new site in El-Alamein in 2019.

might be a bit surprised to be in this precise spot. Although it is in the center of the city, it is in no great square close to royalty or government or power. Parliament and Big Ben can be seen far in the distance, but they are not an integral part of the scene. The location doesn't seem to shout of any great symbolic meaning like it does for many of the locations of the other monoliths. This is a bit surprising, because you'd think London, in its heyday the center of one of the greatest empires of all time, would have been eager to connect itself more directly with the past glory that the obelisk represents.

But then I got back to looking at the river. Therein surely lay this obelisk's uniqueness and the key to its message. It had come from a country that was largely defined by its river. And, to a great extent, it was now standing centuries later alongside a similarly iconic river. When it had first been erected here in 1876, the British Empire was at its peak. Perched atop the new Embankment and bearing witness to the traffic and cargo flowing on the river, making London the richest city in the world, it would have seen similarities with the country of its birth at the time of its initial placement in the city of Heliopolis. Over time, that great "city of the sun" had been abandoned, the obelisk had been toppled, and it had been re-erected centuries later in its new home in Alexandria, one of the most celebrated cities of the Roman Empire. But that city had fallen too, and the obelisk had remained in the dust for centuries until it ended its tumultuous, watery voyage here on the Embankment.

As the years have passed in its new location, the monolith has witnessed many things. It was undoubtedly shocked by the bombings that almost destroyed the city in World War II, and maybe even more shocked that its new home, despite being on the winning side of the war, has almost completely lost its empire. It surely has begun to notice that the river palaces of Hampton Court and Greenwich are now filled with day trippers and not with the rulers of the most powerful nation on earth; that river traffic is not what it used to be, now almost entirely consisting of tourist boats sponsored by companies such as Uber, shuttling vacationers from one tourist attraction to another—a kind of watery Las Vegas strip with the big London Eye Ferris wheel dominating the scene. And finally it undoubtedly has overheard all the recent conversations of passersby talking about Brexit and how the country could possibly become a second- or third-tier power with some of its former colonies surpassing it economically. In fact, the supporters of Brexit have admiringly spoken of the movement as a way to turn London into a "Singapore-on-Thames."

It was telling me it had seen this all before. It was saying that "Ozymandias" wasn't just a tale of the fleeting nature of individual fame and power. It was a tale that pertained to countries and whole empires as well. It knew from experience that no amount of effort or planning would ever prevent this rise, decline, and fall from happening again and again. If we are lucky, all that will survive will be the stories that are told and the meanings they convey.

And the river of time will flow on and on.

▪ ▪ ▪

As with the Central Park Obelisk, buried underneath this one in London is a time capsule. In it are copies of the Bible in several languages, a portrait of Queen Victoria, and a history of the transportation of the monument from Egypt. The capsule's primary contents, however, are simple objects that were typical of the Victorian age, such as some children's toys, a box of cigars, several tobacco pipes, a box of hairpins, a railway guide, and a map of London.

As I stood looking up at the obelisk and contemplated what was buried beneath it, I was struck by the contrast between what man produces today and what he produced in the past, and the difference in mentality it must inevitably reflect. With the obelisk, the Egyptians created something that they thought would last forever. Each one took many years and thousands of workers to produce. Moving an obelisk involved great logistical effort and costs. Such effort reflects the priorities of a society that valued things that were permanent.

Today we have a different mindset. We mass-produce things, many with a deliberately planned obsolescence or with immediate and repeated consumption in mind that requires repurchase and continual production. It all started right here in England with the Industrial Revolution in the nineteenth century. The objects in the time capsule illustrate that. But we have far outstripped the Victorians in our ability (and obsession) to produce more and more "stuff."

I participated in this thinking all of my professional life. Not far from the obelisk south of London is the European headquarters of the division of the global company I once worked for. Throughout the UK in places like Egham and Newcastle are manufacturing facilities I have visited many times—places that produce soap, paper products, shampoo, and other consumer products. They are marvels of technology and high-speed manufacturing. The emphasis is on scale, mass production, speed, turnover. It's the way it has to be if you are in the consumer products business. But it reflects an underlying sensibility that is so different from that of the ancient Egyptians. I suspect they would have approved of making things that would improve their personal appearance. There's enough of their beautiful jewelry that still exists to suggest they would.

But on a deeper level, I bet they would fundamentally not have understood a society that spends most of its time and resources making so much "stuff." Nearby this four-thousand-year-old obelisk are several superstores that stock tens of thousands of SKUs (i.e., individual items), the vast majority of which last little more than a few days, let alone a few weeks. And the one place in the entire world that may best embody the notion of the proliferation of "stuff" is in Knightsbridge, just two miles away from the obelisk: Harrods. Ironically, this store was owned for many years by an Egyptian, the recently deceased Mohamed Al-Fayed. It was under his ownership that the famous Egyptian escalators, complete with their wall renderings of pharaohs and a variety of ancient scenes, were created in the middle of the store, shuttling people from floor to floor overflowing with merchandise.*

I spent my whole career throwing around terminology meant to promote speed and efficiency—phrases like "just-in-time inventory," "product lifecycle," "consumer demand," and "global sourcing." The ancient Egyptians would not have understood any of that.

Obelisks came from one source in Aswan (parts from how many countries does it take to produce one iPhone?) and were meant to last forever. This, over time, cannot help but create vastly different mind-sets and values in societies. We get so deep into these mindsets that we can hardly imagine that life was ever different. We forget that we shaped our world little by little, not always remembering what all the experiences, facts, biases, and assumptions were that led us to shape it this way in the first place.

Can we possibly have anything in common with a people who had such different focus and priorities? Even more, is there anything we can possibly learn from them? Is it mentally healthier to place value in making fewer things meant to last or making many things not intended to last? Does it lead to more or less happiness (admittedly a vague term)? Perhaps there's a balance to be reached here. Maybe we reached

---

* Born in Alexandria, Egypt, Mohamed Al-Fayed and his brother owned Harrods from 1985 to 2010, at which time it was sold to its current owner, the sovereign wealth fund of the Qatar Investment Authority. Among his other investments, he also owned the Hotel Ritz Paris and the Fulham Football Club. His son, Dodi, was in a relationship with Diana, Princess of Wales, when both died in a car crash in Paris in 1997.

it at some previous point in history? Or are we continuing to move in the right direction? These days I tend to think almost instinctively in terms of cycles: that extremes are not good, and pendulums tend to swing too far one way or the other over time.

This obelisk and its time capsule underneath reflect two very different worldviews. It is the permanent versus the throwaway, the eternal versus the temporary. Today we live in "real time." The ancient Egyptians just lived in Time.

The London obelisk on the Thames: the scene today from the Victoria Embankment

Chapter 7

DORSET (ENGLAND): LOST IN TRANSLATION

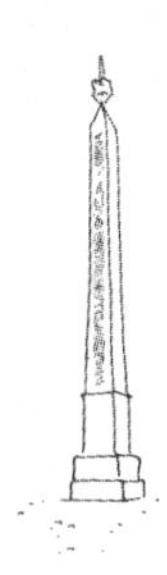

Historical Background

At around 118 BCE, in the reign of the ethnic Greek Pharaoh Ptolemy IX, a pair of obelisks was installed before the temple devoted to the goddess Isis on the island of Philae, near Aswan. They had probably been originally quarried nearby in about 1400 BCE. One of them was moved to Kingston Lacy in 1821. There are several aspects of this monolith that make it different from the other twenty-five.

First, its inscription is not the usual formulaic tribute to various gods, nor does it praise a pharaoh. Instead, it is a direct plea from Egyptian priests to the pharaoh and queen for financial aid. The favorable response and the granting of a tax exemption are also inscribed.

Second, it is the only obelisk to ever have been acquired directly from Egypt by an individual and placed on his private property. On a trip to Egypt in 1815, a wealthy English member of Parliament, amateur explorer, and antiques collector named William John Bankes first saw the monolith before the Temple of Isis (its mate had broken into pieces long before), and in 1819 he arranged for it to be shipped back to his estate, called Kingston Lacy, in the southwestern county of Dorset. The Italian explorer, adventurer, and archaeologist Giovanni Belzoni arranged the move of the obelisk to England at the behest of Bankes. A former circus performer, the six-foot, seven-inch-tall Belzoni is one of the most colorful characters in the era of Egyptomania, having overseen the removal of many ancient Egyptian artifacts to other foreign locales. In 1827 the monolith's current location in the garden behind the Kingston Lacy mansion was selected by the family friend and hero of the Napoleonic Wars, the Duke of Wellington. He presided over the dedicatory ceremonies that year as well.

But there is a third reason that this particular monolith had interested Bankes, and it is that which differentiates it from the other twenty-five. While the inscriptions of all the others are solely in hieroglyph, this Philae obelisk, because it was the only one erected in Egypt after the Macedonian Alexander the Great's conquest of the kingdom, also has an inscription in Greek on its pedestal. This dual-language text was to have enormous consequences.

One of the byproducts of Napoleon's invasion of Egypt was an obsession with translating the confusing markings found on many artifacts, tombs, and temples. No one knew what to make of these strange etchings. Were they individual letters of an alphabet with individual sounds that created words? Or were they pictures that conveyed a complete idea and profound truths? Or some combination of both? For centuries it was assumed that each individual hieroglyph was meant to convey a deep spiritual concept, a sort of a writing of the gods.

But then came the French discovery of the Rosetta Stone in 1799, and the translation race heated up. The French effort was led by the archaeologist Jean-François Champollion. A British polymath named Thomas Young made the first breakthrough in 1814 when he saw a copy of the Rosetta Stone with its three parallel texts: one in hieroglyphs, a second in a script that scholars had named "demotic," and a third in Greek. He correctly determined that demotic was a derivative of hieroglyph and was then able to identify several hieroglyph characters in what he was fairly sure was the name "Ptolemy." Further progress stalled until 1821 when Bankes, in looking at the dual Greek/hieroglyph inscription on his obelisk in Dorset, made an educated guess that he had found the hieroglyphs that spelled "Cleopatra." Bankes widely circulated a lithograph of the hieroglyph/Greek text on his obelisk, noting his "Cleopatra guess" in pencil. Champollion got a copy of this and applied Bankes's guess to the hieroglyphs on the Rosetta Stone. The Cleopatra guess worked, and with two words now deciphered—Ptolemy and Cleopatra—Champollion was able to publish a rough translation of the entire texts on the Rosetta Stone by 1823. The hieroglyph code had been broken.[1]

Champollion never gave due credit to Bankes's contribution, although current scholars are increasingly doing so and sometimes refer to the Philae monolith as a sort of second Rosetta Stone. Moreover, the Rosetta Stone and this obelisk are now linked together forever in the most unlikely of all places: outer space. In 2004 the European Space Agency (ESA) began what it called the Rosetta Mission, the goal of which was to learn more about comets in our solar system. Launched from French Guiana in 2004, the spacecraft *Rosetta* orbited the comet Churyumov-Gerasimenko for seventeen months, and its "lander" reached the nucleus of the comet in 2014 (making it the first craft ever to land on a comet). The ESA team apparently had a keen sense of history, because they named the lander *Philae* after the island in the Nile that was the original home of the Kingston Lacy obelisk. These carefully chosen names were meant to communicate the hope that the spacecraft (*Rosetta*) and the orbiter (*Philae*) would combine to further scientific understanding as did their two Egyptian namesakes with their combined decoding of hieroglyphs. The *Philae* lander is still embedded in this comet, its signal now gone dead, its purpose having been accomplished. But who knows? It would only be fitting if some collector in the distant future were to find their way to this comet lying between Mars and Jupiter, dig it up, and bring it back to their estate, just as Bankes unearthed the *Philae* after it had been abandoned for two thousand years.[2]

Bankes's story ends up being a tragic one. Having been discovered to be homosexual in an era that had no tolerance for it, he was forced to live in exile, beginning in 1841, and to sign his estate over to his brother. Although he continued to ship artifacts back to Kingston Lacy from abroad, he never saw it or the obelisk again.*[3] It remains standing in the garden of Kingston Lacy estate today, which is now a property of the National Trust and can be visited by the public.[4]

Finally, three miles away by foot from the estate through the scenic Dorset countryside lies the quaint village of Colehill. Here once lived Tim Berners-Lee, the inventor of the World Wide Web, often called the Father of the Internet. Using the internet-based hypertext system he had envisioned, he created the first internet website of all time in 1989 at CERN in Geneva, where he was working at the time. Sir Timothy then became the director of the World Wide Web Consortium

---

* Bankes was twice found guilty of having committed homosexual acts. The first was in 1837. He was a member of Parliament and was seen with a young soldier entering a dark corner of London and was arrested for indecent exposure. Bankes claimed that he was urinating, and, despite some well-known character witnesses such as the Duke of Wellington, he was ultimately issued a steep fine and released. But his reputation was severely damaged. Then in 1839 a similar incident occurred, again in London. This time he fled the country before he could be sentenced. He went to live in Venice as what the court called "an outlaw" and was forbidden to enter the country at any time.

(3WC) headquartered at MIT, which helps set the standards for the future development of the web. This and the Philae obelisk make this rural corner of the English countryside the unlikely home of two "code pioneers" whose work has led to two of the biggest breakthroughs in the history of communications.

Impressions and Context

After seeing the London obelisk, I spent another day in town. The next day, I rented a car and began driving south, my ultimate destination being the town of Wimborne Minster in Dorset. I've driven a lot in Europe, but I find England by far the most difficult country to do so, because keeping to the left-hand side of the road demands my full attention. Particularly difficult is shifting gears with the left hand and circling the numerous roundabouts in a clockwise rather than the usual counterclockwise manner. But given the rural location of Dorset, going by car was the only option. My route was a circuitous one, and it would take me a couple of days to reach the Philae obelisk at the estate of Kingston Lacy in Wimborne. I was in no hurry and wanted to visit a few places of antiquity along the way that might shed light on the connection between past and present, especially as it related to the obelisk I was about to visit in Dorset.

My first stop was Stonehenge. This was the third time I'd visited there, and every time the experience changes. The first time was forty-five years previously. In those days you could drive up directly to a parking area very near the stones and literally walk between them. There was little signage, and no guides. It was all experiential and very dramatic. The second time was twenty years later. At that point you had to park in a new lot quite far from the monument, walk a good distance through a tunnel, and then arrive at the circle of stone, which was now roped off. You walked around the perimeter. It was still a dramatic site, but something had been lost.

The approach today is different still. You park very far away at a well-done visitors center with exhibits and information explaining what you will see. You then take a shuttle bus to the stones, where you walk around them in the roped-off perimeter. Tourism here (and elsewhere) has clearly evolved over the years, with an understandable emphasis on preserving antiquity while educating the tourist with more on-site information. Many travel experiences are not nearly as raw as they were in the past. They are more orchestrated, more scripted, which has its pluses and minuses.

For my purposes, there was a particular point of interest for me regarding Stonehenge. Although the ground it stands on shows signs of some landscaping and small building activity going back to 3000 BCE, the circle of stones that we see today with its horizontal lintels dates to 2500 BCE. This makes it one of the very few massive man-made structures on earth still standing that is exactly contemporaneous with the Great Pyramid of Giza and the emergence of the great civilization of ancient Egypt. It invites comparisons between the two civilizations, and that interested me. One can certainly marvel at the ability of the people who created Stonehenge to move those huge stones to their present position in the plains north of Salisbury. (The larger Sarsen stones came from Marlborough Downs, 25 miles away, and the smaller bluestones were brought 160 miles from the Preseli Hills in Wales. Quite an achievement!). But the monument itself cannot compare to the Great Pyramid. It is the most basic of all structures, crudely assembled and reaching a height of 30 feet. On the other hand, the Pyramid stands at 481 feet and is a marvel not only of logistics but of design and architecture. Stonehenge is the product of a primitive people who appear to have had no written language or alphabet and who therefore remain a mystery to us. All we can surmise now is that they had a reverence for the sun, and the monument appears to be constructed as a sort of temple to solar movement. As a result, much of Stonehenge scholarship today is an exercise in astronomical code-breaking based on the seasonal positioning of the sun in relationship to the stone formations. The pyramids were created by a much more advanced civilization that was developing a complex written communication system that has allowed us to understand a good deal about its creators.

The first obelisks were still a few hundred years away from being erected, and they, like Stonehenge, are tributes to the sun. But they are technical marvels too, carefully sculpted, manufactured, and inscribed. They speak to us more directly. Importantly, they are now widely distributed globally, mostly in highly populated areas where they have the capacity to speak daily to a contemporary audience in their modern settings. They have stories to tell. However, Stonehenge stands alone in a vast, empty plain—it is impressive, for sure, but it interacts with no modern environment as do the pyramids and the obelisks. It has no message other than, perhaps, for a few latter-day "Druids," the spiritual descendants of an ancient people that were once thought to have been the builders of Stonehenge but are now uniformly deemed to have had no connection with it. Despite this, modern Druidic practitioners still come. But they are few, and for the rest of the masses that swarm the site, the stones are just a magnificent, silent curiosity—a one-off from everyday life.

▪ ▪ ▪

My next stop in search of antiquity was a bit of a backtrack two hours away in Rochester, a fine small city in the county of Kent. It is known for its cathedral (the second oldest in Britain, dating back to 650) and its Norman castle of 1215. It is also ground zero for Charles

Dickens enthusiasts, as the author lived in and frequented this area his whole life. Being a fan of Dickens, I was delighted to soak in the local color where he set so many of his novels. But in this instance, I was most interested in ancient history, and I was in town in search of a past that predated Dickens, the cathedral, and the castle by thousands of years. I was searching for a tree.

Actually I was searching for a wooden table that was manufactured from a tree that dates back over five thousand years. In 3000 BCE the so-called black oak trees flourished in the East Anglia area of eastern England abutting the North Sea. They were immense. While the oak tree of today stands at a maximum height of fifty feet, the black oaks were almost triple that and must have been thought to be indestructible. But then global warming occurred. The earth's massive ice sheets melted, and the seas rose. The nearby North Sea rose to heights that completely flooded the land that the trees stood upon, causing them to topple. Some, however, were buried deep in the earth, and a few were trapped in airtight pockets that have allowed them to be astonishingly well preserved. One in particular was found a dozen years ago and, through great artistry, was milled into the ten beautiful, full-length planks from which this table was made. It stands inside Rochester Cathedral, rather overlooked. It appears in no tourist write-ups of the cathedral that I found. The plan is for it to move on from there someday to some other yet-to-be-determined location.

It's too bad more publicity isn't given to this table. It was interesting to me, given my project, because it was an example of something I hadn't run across yet or even thought much about: a modern product made very recently from what had been a living organism five thousand years ago. The obelisks came from inert stone. The table was composed of materials that had once been alive, standing taller than the tallest Egyptian obelisk, and then dead for thousands of years. They now have been given a second "life" of their own. Talk about recycling.

But it speaks to another reality, and a worrisome one, that the signage in the cathedral near the table clearly spelled out for me. The East Anglian peoples of 5000 BCE could not have imagined that these mighty trees would be destroyed. But a change in climate that they did not understand and were powerless to impact had wreaked apocalyptic damage. We face potentially similar climatic challenges today. We understand them and know that there are steps we can take. And we are definitely taking dramatic ones. Yet the whole subject is shrouded in controversy, politics, and, worst of all, the culture wars. Lines have been drawn; opponents have been identified. Some people have adopted positions based on a dislike of the other side rather than objective facts. The result is that while much has been accomplished, much more action is needed. If ever there were an issue that threatens everyone, where it should have been relatively easy to reach collegial consensus, it is this one. But we have not done so. On the one hand, we have some individuals who have developed what some in the mental health field are formally identifying as "eco-psychosis"—also referred to as a sort of environmental PTSD. Others completely deny the climate problem. How could this have happened? How can there be such a large gulf between people? Is tribalism so deeply ingrained in us that it continues to overwhelm undeniable fact?

Beyond DNA, there must be something else at work today that is amplifying the basic tendency for mankind to form into tribes. What is this amplifier?

This question was on my mind the next morning as I pulled into Kingston Lacy. Its obelisk ended up shedding some light on this question.

▪ ▪ ▪

Kingston Lacy was the estate of the Bankes family dating back to the 1600s. Today it is owned and managed by the National Trust.

I paid to enter the property of the estate and took a guided tour of the mansion, learning much more about the life of the Bankes family and its most famous member, William Joseph Bankes. A friend of Byron at Cambridge, a member of Parliament, a traveler to then-obscure parts of the world, the second European ever to visit Petra, and the assembler of a great art collection that still exists, he is one of the most interesting people I ran into in the pursuit of obelisks. (His exciting life, along with its sad and undeserved ending in exile in Venice, is told in the excellent book *The Exiled Collector*, by Anne Sebba.) After the house tour, I made for the garden where the monolith stands.

The Philae obelisk, with a height of twenty-two feet, is not the biggest or most impressive of the twenty-six, but it gets my vote as one of the most thought-provoking. While many of the obelisks speak to us in a hushed voice, their message for a modern audience needing to be coaxed out of them, this obelisk speaks loudly to us. Unlike the other obelisks, the words inscribed on it are a direct message to us. It is this obelisk's role with the Rosetta Stone in deciphering hieroglyphs that gives clarity to its voice.

The deciphering of the hieroglyphs had proven to be a surprisingly difficult task. After the initial euphoria of finding the Rosetta Stone in 1799, twenty years went by without much progress. It was still unknown whether the hieroglyphs were letters, words, or pictures of concepts, or if they were meant to be read left to right or up or down. The characters were all in a continuous block, with no spacing or punctuation. And it was not related to any other language.

But between this obelisk and the Rosetta Stone, the code had been cracked. An ancient civilization that had never been able to communicate to later ones now came into focus and could be understood. A link to an earlier stage of human thought had been found. The combined work of Champollion, Bankes, and Young had been a great example of codebreaking done in the interest of promoting a common understanding of something.

It was the pursuit of this theme of decoding and deciphering that had drawn me to visit Bletchley Park after I had seen the London obelisk two days previously. Its campus-like location lies a forty-five-minute train ride north of London. It was here, during World War II, that an eclectic group of individuals, many of them women, solved the riddle of the Germans' Enigma machines, which were ciphering devices used to pass along secret messages in code. Early versions of computers developed by the Poles and the English were key, the most famous of which was the electromagnetic device known as the Bombe, the brainchild of the mathematician Alan Turing. The German code was essentially a language based on mathematics that a computer like the Bombe was able to ultimately solve. Some of the funding for the maintenance of Bletchley has come from Google in honor of the park's role in the development of the modern computer. It had helped develop a new medium of communication.

Codes, deciphering, extracting meaning from unfamiliar words. It got me thinking. Words have traditionally been constructs we use to describe some aspect of reality to promote a common understanding of it. Today they have become sellable commodities that often promote narrow thinking and division. Our primary medium today is the internet. We use it to communicate, to entertain, to learn, to compute, to work. It is the repository of an infinite number of our words, thoughts, ideas. And all of the above are now being sold. They all have a price. And somebody or something is buying them. Companies are increasingly skewing ad budgets toward internet word and behavior acquisition, all in the hopes of creating their own analytical "secret sauce" or code to place people into demographics—or, to use an even trendier term, psychographic—"buckets" in order to "target" them for marketing purposes. The buckets include gender, religion, political party, habits, practices, preferences, hopes, and fears. Buckets mean separation and division.

I've been party to all of this, and I've become increasingly disturbed by the direction it is heading in. Political parties, governments, and hate groups are now in the game and are paying real money for all of this. And the big game changer is artificial intelligence. AI gets better the more it learns about something. And how does it learn? By scraping the internet and its infinite amount of content, much of which is linked to the specific individual who knowingly or unknowingly sold it to some third, fourth, or fifth party. All of our words that we've allowed some seller to sell to some nameless buyer could, depending on the buyer's intent, create major problems. There are a number of smart people who are saying we are creating a monster.

It didn't need to be this way. We are where we are because the internet was set up as a "free" network that always depended on its users' selling chunks of their privacy to interested buyers. There are ways around this, ways that allow users to maintain their privacy. For all its dangers and flaws, the cryptocurrency model is a platform that addresses this. At its core is a kind of alternative to the internet model. But it's probably too late to hope for much change, and certainly cryptocurrency is not the ideal spokesperson for what is its interesting underlying technology, blockchain.

So here's where my visit to the Philae monolith left me. This obelisk is a powerful embodiment of codebreaking that has helped us to understand the mentality of a civilization very different from our own. It connects us back to the earliest recorded days of our species, and we can contemplate what we've gained or lost over time. Indeed, it has even become something of a symbol that promotes the attainment of common knowledge through teamwork and partnership, as the naming of the *Philae* lander after it will attest. Further, at Bletchley Park, we broke codes and deciphered meaning to end a war and to gain a peace. Visit the place, and it exudes camaraderie and a commitment to commonly held ideals. All good.

But today we decipher to categorize people, to group them into defined tribes that can be targeted by interested parties, or to solidify tribal boundaries to the exclusion of others. The Philae obelisk breaks down barriers between peoples, times, and places. Our new media, despite its awesome potential to further break some barriers down, is moving in the direction of building some new ones. Maybe this is not so good.

Perhaps this is an example of the law of unintended consequences at work. And maybe all of this is now inevitable. In any case, what it will mean is the proliferation of clearly defined tribes. It will be easier for them to be formed around more and more issues. The rhetoric will grow more polarizing, with groups yelling more and more loudly at each other and understanding each other less and less.

. . .

What makes the Philae obelisk so interesting to me is that it not only helps to tell the story of an entire civilization like its twenty-five other mates. This one also speaks to me about my personal past. The monolith's positive role in the history of communication points the finger at me, puts my own actions into a wider perspective. During the course of my business career, in my own very small way, I was aligned with efforts to place people into buckets, cohorts, tribes—whatever you want to call them. It was smartest-guy-in-the-room stuff. It showed an analytical mind. It made you feel cutting-edge. It had a lingo all of its own. It was fairly innocuous stuff at the time, and most of it still largely is. You can even talk yourself into believing that by buying as much of their identity as the law allows you to, you are doing people a service by matching products and information they will find useful to them. But there's also the knowledge that at a minimum, you've financially enabled a system to flourish that encourages thinking of people as stereotypes. And at its worst, it has helped spawn the growth of a tribalism that leads to actions that haven't always been quite so innocent.

Hearing the message of a 2,500-year-old codebreaking obelisk that stands near the former home of the Father of the Internet had prompted me to do some contemplating. A "contemplative man of leisure" is yet another oxymoron. I was beginning to make a habit of this, and I wasn't sure I liked it. Perhaps the odyssey pendulum was swinging too far to the "purpose" side and needed to move back more to the "fun" side.

My next stop would be the perfect place to do it: Italy.

The Philae obelisk on the Kingston Lacy estate in Dorset, depicted with other codebreaking pioneers

PART III

THE OBELISKS OF THE FORMER ROMAN EMPIRE: ITALY AND TURKEY

In which the ancient past and the personal present are brought ever-closer together, in lands where la dolce vita, art, and some of man's greatest achievements all too often collide with grim realities

Background

The Roman passion for Egypt began in 48 BCE, when Julius Caesar first led his powerful army into Alexandria and defeated the Egyptians. He set Cleopatra and her brother up as pharaohs, became her lover, and fathered a child. She went to live in Rome for a period as well.

In 31 BCE, Octavian defeated the joint forces of Mark Antony and Cleopatra and officially made the territory a part of the Roman Empire. Octavian (now Caesar Augustus) valued Egypt for its

agricultural resources, which provided the empire with much of its grain, cotton, papyrus, and other essential products. But he was also enamored with Egypt's place in history and wanted to align himself with it to buttress his own image as a mighty leader and godlike figure.

So he started importing obelisks to Rome. The monoliths made a dramatic visual impression on the common man or woman; they could be moved (with some effort) to be placed strategically throughout the city for maximum effect, and they helped him tell his story that the Roman Empire was the direct descendant of Egypt, and he of the omnipotent pharaohs. In 10 BCE he exported his first two obelisks from Egypt to Rome.

Many other emperors followed suit. By the fourth century CE, it is said that over fifty obelisks in Rome alone had been erected at various points in time. Many had subsequently fallen, but some were re-erected later, many by popes as a tribute to Jesus Christ. The upshot of it is that today there are twenty ancient obelisks still standing in lands of the former Roman Empire.

But we need to clarify something first regarding what is and isn't an Egyptian obelisk. For an obelisk to be deemed truly Egyptian, many experts say (and I have adopted this criterion here), it must have three elements: it must come from the quarries of Aswan, it must have been commissioned by a pharaoh, and it must have been initially erected in Egypt. With this definition, we can say there are eleven full-fledged Egyptian obelisks in the lands of the former Roman Empire—ten in Italy, one in Turkey. Nine other obelisks still stand in these lands, and although ancient and interesting, they are not truly Egyptian. Six of these "pseudo-Egyptian" monoliths are in Italy (five in Rome, one in Benevento), one in France (Arles), one in

Turkey (Istanbul), and one in Israel (in the Caesaria Maritima archaeological zone north of Tel Aviv).

ITALY

Italy has ten that can be classified as fully Egyptian.

1. Rome: Piazza di Montecitorio (Solarium obelisk)
2. Rome: Piazza del Popolo (Flaminio obelisk)
3. Rome: Viale delle Terme di Diocleziano (Dogali obelisk)
4. Rome: St. Peter's Square (Vatican obelisk)
5. Rome: Piazza di San Giovanni in Laterano
6. Rome: Piazza della Rotonda (the San Macuteo obelisk)
7. Rome: Villa Mattei (Celimontana obelisk)
8. Rome: Piazza della Minerva
9. Florence: Boboli Gardens
10. Urbino: Piazza del Rinascimento

TURKEY

One Egyptian obelisk is found in Istanbul, which, when it was the capital of the eastern Roman Empire, was called Constantinople.

Technically my odyssey includes only these ten obelisks in Italy and the one in Turkey. However, in order to complete the picture, I have briefly summarized some facts on the other nine "pseudo-Egyptian" obelisks in the Afterword. I have seen all but one, and each one is interesting in its own right.

All these obelisks are connected in some way to the power of empire. Some speak to religious authority or spirituality also, still others to art. And many of the Italian ones, because of their locations, have a la dolce vita element to them today.

■ ■ ■

One final thought before moving on. Rome is the next stop, which, in my mind, is the best city on earth to walk idly through. I'd love to find the Italian word for *flaneur*. But alas, there doesn't seem to be an exact equivalent. My online research comes up with *camminatore*, which literally means "walker." Yes, flaneuring is walking, but it's more than that. It's a devil-may-care, world-weary strolling around. *Walker* sounds too focused, like walking your dog, power walking for exercise, or walking to the corner drugstore to pick up a prescription. Too much purpose, not enough idle fun.

So I'm going to use another word my English-to-Italian dictionary is pushing me toward. I know it's not quite right, but I like it anyhow. The word is *vagabondo*. Yes, it can mean a "hobo" (I wasn't quite that—at least not yet). Worse, it's a close synonym for another Italian word, *barbone*, which means "bum" (again, I hope I'm not that, although some people I know would say I'm closer to a bum than a hobo). But I'm going to stick with *vagabondo* under the belief that putting an *o* at the end makes it a tad more stylish and continental. So when you read some of the more serious observations in the next few chapters, please consider that the author walking the streets has no aspirations to be a scholar. Think of him as someone who has a sweater draped casually (but strategically) across his shoulders, the sleeves tied carefully just below the neck, imagining that is the way debonair actors such as Marcello Mastroianni and Rossano Brazzi, or the dapper former goalkeeper of Juventus, Gigi Buffon, do it.

Andiamo avanti!

Chapter 8

ROME: THE OBELISKS OF EMPIRE

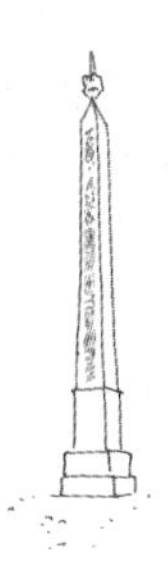

The Solarium Obelisk (in Piazza di Montecitorio)

The Flaminio Obelisk (in Piazza del Popolo)

Historical Background

These are the first two obelisks ever removed from Egypt. Both relocations were done by order of Caesar Augustus, and both came from the once great city of Heliopolis, which by 10 BCE was an abandoned ruin. Both bear the same inscription: "Augustus, son of divine Caesar, dedicated this obelisk to the sun when Egypt had been brought under the sway of the Roman people." In other words, these two are trophies of empire, commemorating Augustus's conquest of Egypt.

The obelisk in Piazza Montecitorio (also called the Solarium obelisk) was raised in Heliopolis during the reign of Pharaoh Psammetichus

II (595–589 BCE) and erected by Augustus in the so-called Campus Martius in the center of Rome. Interestingly, it served as the vertical shaft (known as a gnomen) of a giant sundial. It was placed so that the shadow of the sun would fall on the monument Ara Pacis, dedicated to honor the emperor precisely on his birthday of September 23. The obelisk and Ara Pacis stand near the Mausoleum of Augustus, where the emperor is buried. According to the *Cambridge Ancient History*, the proximity of the three structures presented a "collective message that dramatically linked peace with military authority and imperial expansion."[1]

The monolith fell at some point, was discovered, and was re-erected in 1792 by Pope Pius VI in front of a building that housed the papal courts. Today the building is called the Palazzo Montecitorio and is the seat of the Chamber of Deputies (Italy's lower house of Parliament).

The obelisk in Piazza del Popolo (also called the Flaminio obelisk) was inscribed in the reigns of Pharaoh Seti I (1294–1279 BCE) and Ramesses II (1279–1213 BCE), raised in Heliopolis, and subsequently erected by Augustus in the middle of the Circus Maximus. In the Circus, chariot races were held, and the chariots' racing counterclockwise around the obelisk was meant to be a metaphor for the cosmos. Augustus was being linked to the sun as the center of the universe, a further and very intentional reinforcement of his divinity. He would become officially deified after his death.[2]

The Flaminio obelisk eventually toppled and was excavated and re-erected by Pope Sixtus V in the Piazza del Popolo in 1589. It was so placed because this piazza is a major entryway into Rome, and several key roads branch out from there. In the late 1700s, Pope Pius VI wanted the piazza redesigned, a project that was finally undertaken by the architect Giuseppe Valadier in the 1820s. His redesign included the entire Pincian Hill behind the Piazza, which is linked to it by winding stairs and terraces.

Impressions and Context

Given that these two obelisks represent the first two monoliths ever shipped out of Egypt, I planned my itinerary so that I could see them consecutively. That's not difficult to do, since they are only a fifteen-minute walk from each other.

In their original locations in the time of Augustus, it would have been easy to see how they furthered his narrative as the one divine, mighty ruler of a great empire. The Solarium sundial monolith's being positioned smack-dab in the center of Campus Martius clearly spoke of Rome's military might. And with its proximity to two of the most prominent monuments to Augustus, the Ara Pacis and his mausoleum, he would have been personally linked to ancient power and divinity. So too with the Flaminio obelisk. Being at the center of the Circus Maximus and its chariots spinning around it (note to self: see *Ben Hur* again), this monolith dedicated to him would have put him at the center of the cosmos—a sun king, so to speak.

But neither obelisk is in its original location. The Flaminio is now in the busy Piazza del Popolo. Thank goodness car traffic has been prohibited since 1997, and it's easy to walk up to it. And the Solarium is now in the piazza that fronts the Italian lower house of Parliament. Although the two monoliths are tall and majestic structurally, neither screams "empire" specifically in its current location. But if you take a ten-minute walk and widen your perspective, the two of them begin to speak.

Start in front of the Flaminio and walk across the Piazza del Popolo to where the Via del Corso starts. This is Rome's main street, its version of Fifth Avenue. It runs about 1.5 miles, straight as an arrow, and ends at the huge white monument to King Victor Emmanuel on the Piazza Venezia (officially called the "Vittoriano," but more commonly referred to as "The Wedding Cake"). Walk about ten minutes down the Via del Corso, and you come to the Piazza Colonna and stop there. That's where the story is.

If you move to the far side of this piazza, you can begin to see the Solarium obelisk in front of the Italian Parliament building one hundred yards away. If you stand on the Corso side of the Piazza and look right, you can see the Flaminio obelisk you just walked from. If you look straight down the Corso to your left, you can make out the gigantic Vittoriano monument complex about another ten-minute walk from where you are. And across from the monument is the Piazza Venezia and the ducal palazzo where Mussolini would stand on his balcony and work the crowd into a frenzy.

This spot provides a unique perspective from which to contemplate the various stages of autocracy and empire and its alternatives. You start with the two obelisks of Augustus and all they imply regarding conquest in the imperial age. You then turn to see the gradual evolution of Italy into a modern state in the nineteenth century, with a huge monument dedicated to Victor Emmanuel II, the first king of a unified Italy, whose powers by that time could no longer be absolute. Near it, at the Piazza Venezia, you see the headquarters of the twentieth-century fascist demagogue who, we must remember, was elected democratically. Democracy and equality had been embraced by the people, at least in theory. But this went off the rails with il Duce enacting racial laws, aligning himself with Hitler, and trying to establish a latter-day empire of his own with attempts to colonize much of eastern Africa. He openly saw himself as a leader in the mold of Augustus. Back to the past.

And then you turn to look at the Solarium obelisk in front of the parliament building and see that it all ends rather happily in a twenty-first-century democracy with checks and balances. And my goodness, are there ever checks and balances in democracy Italian-style. All you need to do is look at the other building that the obelisk stands in front of to be reminded of that: the Palazzo Chigi. This is where the Italian prime minister lives. It is Italy's White House. Since the end of World War II, the country has had forty-five different administrations. Contrast that with the United States, which has had twenty-one presidential administrations in the same period, and the UK, which has had eighteen prime minister administrations. Italy's prime ministers come and go. Many of them come back again. Some come back multiple times. It's dizzying. Almost none are remembered by the average American, except for maybe Aldo Moro, who was kidnapped for fifty-five days and killed by the Red Brigades in 1978. Or Silvio "Bunga Bunga" Berlusconi, who ushered in an era of bombastic leadership in the 1990s, a trend that seems to be continuing today in democracy in the West. Contrast that with Augustus, who ruled for forty-one years. France holds the record for emperor longevity. Louis XIV ruled for seventy-two years followed by his son Louis XV, who ruled for fifty-eight. Two heads of state in 131 years! The rulers of empires were almost permanent fixtures. Such longevity often did not translate into much improvement in the lives of the average person.

From Roman Empire to monarchy to democracy-turned-dictatorship and finally to a true—if a sometimes messy—democracy. It's the evolution of man's political thinking from the earliest days up to the present day, complete with occasionally disturbing backsliding that bears our constant attention.

The Solarium obelisk standing in front of the Palazzo Montecitorio (the Italian lower house of Parliament): from autocracy to imperialism to democracy

It's all there to be seen in one fell swoop if we just follow the two ancient obelisks from Aswan standing today near the Via del Corso.

* * *

To complete my walk and to get one final dose of empire, I headed up the Corso until I reached the Via dei Fori Imperiali on the left and took a stroll up it for the umpteenth time. Mussolini knocked down an entire cluttered neighborhood to create a street that would provide an eye-popping vista of the Colosseum. It stares you right in the face at the end of the Via, and it never fails to impress. As you walk, you pass the forums of so many imperial names: Augustus, Julius Caesar, Trajan, and others. You want empire? You got it here, baby.

The images that always come to mind when I walk this street are the victory parades that were held here for every returning conqueror. Titus and the fall of Jerusalem, Caesar with Cleopatra in tow and the annexation of Egypt, Trajan and his many conquests that led to the empire's largest territorial extent by the time of his death. All of them and many more were celebrated here. But with all the pomp that must have accompanied these celebrations, there was always an unassuming figure present at them that speaks well of the Romans' sense of perspective. In the lead chariot stood the conqueror, soaking in the adulation of the adoring crowd. But next to him stood an individual whispering something in the conqueror's ear. Here's how General George Patton famously put it: "For over a thousand years Roman conquerors returning from the wars enjoyed the honor of triumph, a tumultuous parade. But a slave stood behind the conqueror, holding a golden crown and whispering in his ear a warning: that all glory is fleeting."[3]

Seems like good perspective to me, and it's an image I'd love to see at the rallies of some of our current politicians who constantly trumpet their own greatness.

* * *

It was dusk now, and I was ready to head out to dinner. But I had one final thought as I exited the Via dei Fori Imperiali, and it was not of an imperial nature. When I first lived in Rome in 1990, you could park alongside this street. Over time, however, more and more ruins have been discovered, and the archaeological sites along the street have been significantly expanded and have squeezed out the parking areas. Further, the decades-long construction of the badly needed Line C of the Roman Metro has created an immense work zone, making vehicular travel along the Via impractical. Indeed, except for taxis, cars have been banned completely, and this is an extremely good thing. I must confess, though, that a part of me is pretty sad that the era when Gregory Peck could drive Audrey Hepburn down this street and around the Arch of Constantine on a motor scooter in *Roman Holiday* is gone forever. Damn sad indeed ...

The Obelisk of the Baths of Diocletian (also called Dogali)

The Facts

Sometime in the reign of Ramesses II (circa 1250 BCE) this twenty-seven-foot-high monolith was raised in Heliopolis. The Roman emperor Claudius brought it to Rome around 50 CE and erected it in the Iseum, the temple to Isis, the Egyptian goddess whom some Romans had begun to worship. At some point it toppled, became buried for centuries, was excavated, and then was erected in front of the big central train station in Rome in 1887. It was dedicated to the nearly 510 Italian soldiers who were either killed or wounded in Ethiopia at the Battle of Dogali. When the train station was remodeled, it was moved a few hundred yards behind the station, close to the Baths of Diocletian. These baths date to the reign of that emperor in the third century CE and were the largest in Rome. They are now the site of the very fine National Museum of Rome.

Impressions and Context

I wanted one more look at empire after my walk down the Corso, and so the next day I made my way over to the general area of the Stazione Termini to seek out this obelisk. It provides a very different take on this subject.

In its current setting, this obelisk does not send a message of "empire." It stands just off the massive Piazza della Repubblica, a rather nondescript little park that is not particularly well maintained. The monolith is just kind of there. Yet it has a unique pedigree that places it in the "empire" classification, and in a very ironic way.

For one thing, because it is near the Diocletian baths, it is now associated with that rather enigmatic emperor. He was a military leader from Dalmatia (today's Croatia) who was elected emperor because of his prowess in battle. He spent virtually no time in Rome but rather spent his days in the field consolidating Roman territory, particularly in Eastern Europe.

Perhaps its most interesting point is that this obelisk is dedicated to the soldiers killed in Dogali. This was a true battle for empire, but a poorly conceived latter-day one. It was instigated by the Italian King Umberto I, who wanted desperately to establish Italian colonies in Africa. He invaded the Horn of Africa in the 1880s and conquered parts of Somalia and Eritrea. But in 1887 he met surprising resistance at the town of Dogali, where he suffered a humiliating defeat. The battle is often considered to be the first time an African nation defeated a European power. The Italian population was distraught, and so this monolith was quickly excavated and, in an emotional ceremony, dedicated to the fallen.[4]

The debacle at Dogali was not the end of Italy's empire aspirations in Africa. It was the beginning. In 1895 it launched a full-scale invasion of the Horn called the First Italo-Ethiopian War. Italy was again defeated. But it didn't stop there. In 1935 Mussolini again invaded and, after a two-year struggle, succeeded in establishing the Italian Colony of East Africa, which included Ethiopia (then called Abyssinia), Eritrea, and parts of Somalia. In his hubris, he even shipped back to Rome a third-century CE Abyssinian obelisk that was standing at Axum, the ancient Ethiopian town with deep ties to early Christianity that claims one of its churches houses the Ark of the Covenant. Il Duce erected it in a central piazza near the Circus Maximus and directly in front of the headquarters of the Italian African Ministry. But starting in 1941 and until Italy's ultimate defeat in World War II, Ethiopia began to recapture its lands. In 1947 it was formally recognized as an independent state by Italy. Its dreams of an Italian empire in Africa over forever, the Italian government, in 1947, agreed in principle to send the obelisk back to Ethiopia. It finally did so in 2005, shipping it back by air in several pieces in what was described by the BBC as the largest, heaviest object ever transferred by air.[5]

So the Dogali obelisk occupies a unique niche as a symbol of empire. The Flaminio and Solarium obelisks of Augustus are in iconic locations today and present themselves as majestic, if transitory, symbols of empire. The Dogali obelisk, on the other hand, represents an empire that never quite was. Much smaller than its Flaminio and Solarium counterparts, it stands in a humble way in an unassuming park with the names of the Dogali dead inscribed on a commemorative plaque on its base. In this sense it is a bit like the obelisks in Tahrir Square and the Place de la Concorde that honor others who have died. But unlike these two, the Dogali does not commemorate those who died in a profoundly significant event with worldwide implications, like the French Revolution or the Arab Spring. Instead it honors those in a largely forgotten battle in a foolish war that is an example of weakness and not strength. It stands for a mistake.

The Dogali obelisk, then, is little more than a war memorial, a bigger, more ancient version than what can be seen in every cemetery in the world. It fails to project any element of awe or power, but is rather a symbol of senseless death at the hands of foolish and selfish leaders.

In that sense, it has a lot to say about empire.

▪ ▪ ▪

Seen from one vantage point, the area around the obelisk is unattractive—a bit of a wasteland frequented primarily by people who look to be a bit down on their luck, and with the huge train station looming in the background. But from another angle the view is striking, because across the street from the obelisk, on the north side of the Piazza della Repubblica, is the huge Basilica of Santa Maria degli Angeli e dei Martiri, the entirety of which was built into the frigidarium* of the Baths of Diocletian in 1562. The basilica, originally designed by Michelangelo, was the official state church of the Kingdom of Italy between 1870 and 1946, and, in addition to some beautifully excavated rooms from the old baths in its rear portions, it contains a couple of very interesting elements that are relevant to a discussion of obelisks.

The first element is a meridian† created in the interior of the church by order of Pope Clement XI in 1702. His objective was partly

* A frigidarium is a cold room in a typical Roman bath and sometimes contains a swimming pool.

† The first "prime" meridian was set by Eratosthenes in 200 BCE, who became the head of the great Library of Alexandria and was responsible for several

scientific (to prove the accuracy of the Gregorian calendar) and partly political (to one-up the meridian already in place in a church in Bologna). The Santa Maria degli Angeli meridian is fascinating, consisting of a small hole in the church wall, called an oculus, that projects a ray of the sun into the church and onto a forty-five-meter bronze line in the floor. The line and oculus are situated so that the sun ray hits the bronze solar line at noon throughout the year. The way it works is well explained by storyboards off to the side.

The second element in the church is a sixteen-foot bronze statue of Galileo erected in 2010 and designed by Tsung-Dao Lee, a Chinese physicist and Nobel Prize winner. It is called "The Divine Man" and stands in the excavated rooms of the Diocletian baths in the back of the basilica. It is very fitting that this tribute to Galileo is situated directly across the street from an Egyptian obelisk, a structure which embodies a people's belief in the centrality of the sun in their lives. Millennia later, Galileo made a similar point but in a scientific way, championing the Copernican theory of heliocentricity. For this he ran afoul of Pope Urban VIII and was tried and condemned for "vehement suspicion of heresy." An Inquisition tribunal found that heliocentricism is "a proposition which is philosophically absurd and false, and formally heretical, for being explicitly contrary to Holy Scripture."[6] The tribunal and pope ultimately sentenced Galileo to house arrest for the rest of his life.

Then comes the irony: in 1702 Pope Clement XI proudly creates in this majestic basilica his elaborate meridian, a concept which totally depends on the heliocentricity that Galileo championed and for which the church punished him. Finally in 1992, Pope John Paul II officially apologized for the way Galileo was vilified. Better late than never.

At the end of the day, the instinct of the ancient Egyptians to put the sun at the center of their belief system turned out to be closer to

---

scientific breakthroughs, including being the first person to measure the circumference of the earth.

reality than the teachings of the Church leaders of the Renaissance. They saw such centricity as a threat to their literal interpretation of the creation story as told in the Bible.

Superstition and myth based on misguided belief often die hard. There is evidence of this today, although we seem to differ on what is myth and what is truth. And therein lies a big—and growing—problem.

Chapter 9

ROME: THE OBELISKS OF RELIGION

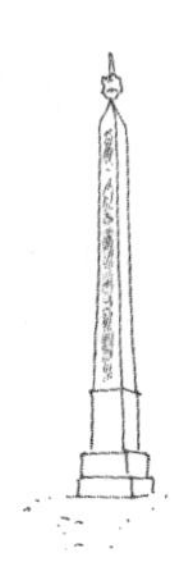

The Vatican Obelisk (St. Peter's Square)

Historical Background

Tiberius succeeded Augustus as emperor. He did not import any obelisks. He showed no affinity for things Egyptian, even banning Egyptian religious rites. But things changed with his successor, Caligula. He was a major follower of the cult of Isis, occasionally dressing in female clothing and wearing a wig in his role as a priest in the cult (there is evidence that he cross-dressed for other reasons too). Many scholars attribute to him the creation of the Iseum, the shrine in Rome which would be the initial destination for many of the obelisks that were imported by future emperors. He, like Augustus, wanted to lay claim to the divine right to rule, which motivated him to follow in his illustrious predecessor's footsteps and import an obelisk.

The monolith he chose had originally been in Heliopolis and now stood in Alexandria. It is impossible to determine which pharaoh first raised it, because it is completely without inscription, the largest monolith without any hieroglyphs whatsoever. In 37 CE, Caligula shipped the obelisk from Alexandria to a chariot oval, or circus, that he was creating near the gardens of his mother Agrippina on the Vaticanus, a small hill in Rome initially settled by the Etruscans. He dedicated it to Augustus and Tiberius.

There it stood for 1,500 years. Then in 1586, Pope Sixtus V got involved. This pope was responsible for reigniting the passion in Rome for obelisks and set about resurrecting many of them that were lying in ruin around the city. His motive was to repurpose the monoliths "for the honor of Christ and his Cross." He therefore decided to move Caligula's obelisk to the Square of St. Peter in front of the new, improved version of the old fourth-century church of that name that had recently been totally rebuilt there. It was a major logistics effort to do so. First the scaffolding had to be designed, along with a series of pulleys and levers. These were then used to remove the obelisk from its current pedestal, "roll" it to its new location, and then raise it onto its new pedestal. It took six months to complete the move of only three hundred yards.[1]

The final step was to "Christianize" a monument that was blatantly pagan. On top was placed a cross. And just so everyone got the message, the new pedestal has the following Latin inscriptions on all four sides:

- On the north side is a dedication by Sixtus V to "The Invincible Cross."
- On the south side it says how Sixtus moved the monolith "dedicated to the wicked cult of heathen gods, with great toil and labor into the precincts of the Apostles."

- The east side exhorts "those who are hostile to the Cross to flee, for the Lion of the tribe of Judah conquers."
- The west side proclaims Christ as ruler and conqueror who protects his followers from evil.

The obelisk stands in this spot in St. Peter's Square today. It is the only obelisk in Italy that has never fallen or needed to be pieced back together from fragments. Some claim this is because it has been a witness to the martyrdom of St. Peter and therefore has had divine protection.

Impressions and Context

I've been to St. Peter's Square many times before and often stood close to the obelisk in the center of it. It must be the most famous and most photographed of all the monoliths. But now that I had been to Egypt, I wanted to pay it another visit and look at the scene through a slightly different lens.

It is positioned in the center of Bernini's colonnaded square in front of Michaelangelo's church and looks out across the Via della Conciliazione, with its swarms of people walking down it to gather in the square. As always, it was an impressive, beautiful, historical, awe-inspiring, and welcoming scene. I also thought it was kind of strange that an Egyptian monolith was in the middle of it.

Its position here in the most sacred spot in all of Christianity makes it the strangest of all bedfellows. For one thing, it was brought to this area by Caligula, the most depraved, immoral emperor of all time, and that's saying a lot right there. And no amount of latter-day pro-Christian writing on its pedestal can negate the fact that this monolith was initially created as a tribute to the pagan sun god Ra by a pharaoh who would not have had the slightest use for the precepts of the Catholic Church or a person like Christ. Not necessarily the most appropriate entree to the square.

There are, however, some points of convergence between the monolith's pagan Egyptian past and its hyper-Christian Roman present. First, as noted in an earlier chapter, the monotheism of both Judaism and Christianity has Egyptian roots that can be directly traced back to Akhenaten. His belief in one supreme being and creator precedes Abraham and the Jewish patriarchs, and his influence can be seen directly in the Old Testament in Psalm 104, which unmistakably echoes his Song to Aten.[2] Although this obelisk was not commissioned by him, neither does it carry any pagan inscription on it, and in that sense it stands in no direct ideological conflict with its Christian surroundings.

There is another point of parallelism between the monolith and its surroundings. This obelisk was raised by two mighty rulers, first an unknown pharaoh in Heliopolis and then Caligula in 37 CE in Rome. Both had absolute power, and both were considered the earthly representative of a divinity. Then in 1586 along comes Pope Sixtus V, another ruler with his own sort of absolute power, and a direct representative of a deity to boot. He re-erects this monolith yet again (and many others elsewhere) and dedicates it to his deity in the tradition that all pharaohs did for theirs.

Is it a stretch to compare popes with pharaohs and emperors? Perhaps a bit, but not entirely. Let's remember that the Vatican is a sovereign state, and the pope is both its political and religious leader. He has unquestioned authority in both. On the temporal side, he is a true head of state. The Vatican has always operated as a politically independent entity, first as the Papal States and then as the city-state of the Vatican. The latter was codified in the Lateran Treaty of 1929. When the modern Italian state was founded in 1870, the Papal States were eliminated and were folded into the new country. But the

Lateran Treaty re-established the independence of Vatican City and the pope as its sovereign leader. He rules for his lifetime and has an aristocracy (the cardinals) and hierarchy similar to dukes and barons (bishops and priests) that support him. As a temporal ruler, he's maybe more of a king than a pharaoh.

But it's on the spiritual side that he becomes closer to a pharaoh or Roman emperor in the mold of Augustus. He is in a direct line from St. Peter, who Christ himself said was his representative on earth. Indeed, the upshot of this is that the pope is granted infallible power in matters of faith. Infallible. That's a pretty strong statement. Even kings don't claim that. And while history is full of monarchs who have been overthrown and exiled by their people or nobility, that has never once happened to a pope. Two have left office (Celestine V in 1294 and Benedict XVI in 2013), but those were voluntary resignations and for reasons of mental or physical health. And finally, in terms of succession, a pope attains his rule not through heredity, as do many monarchical systems, but by the acclaim of his aristocracy, as did the vast majority of Roman emperors and the pharaohs when dynasties changed hands.

I mean no disrespect in comparing popes to monarchs, emperors, and pharaohs. Most have undoubtedly been men of deep faith and have been motivated by the highest ideals. Some have not, however. And motivation and personal behavior aside, the circumstances of how they attain their position, the terms under which they rule, and the power they traditionally have had for most of their two-thousand-year history make them look positively imperial. It makes the positioning of an Egyptian obelisk in the dead center of papal authority very appropriate, and in a way that Sixtus never intended. No other surviving religion in the world today has a figure resembling the pope. But if we look backward in time, we see there is a line of sight between that role and that of the imperial leader of the past.

But things have changed in recent times. The fact is that many Catholics today pay no attention whatsoever to papal decrees or the exhortations of church hierarchy. On the one hand, that's too bad when those exhortations are on solid moral and humanitarian grounds, as they often have been. On the other hand, one can think of more than a few examples when they have not been. In those cases, ignoring the pope and the Church hierarchy has been the right thing to do. In fact it's been downright holy to do so.

Sixtus's inscriptions on the obelisk proclaim that the old majestic hierarchy was being replaced by a majestic new one—one that would conquer opponents. His is a language of conflict, of hostility. I think that this is the wrong message. It is the language a pharaoh would have used. And I'm pretty sure it's not the way Christ himself would have said it.

Such were my impressions that day.

A Memory

The scene is St. Peter's Square, April 19, 2005. It is a sunny day, and the piazza that Bernini designed looks even more spectacular than usual. His two beautiful fountains on either side of the obelisk are bubbling and reflecting the sun. The white colonnade majestically rings the elliptical shape of the piazza, which is filled with people. So too is the Via della Conciliazione, all the way to the Castel Sant'Angelo. There are hundreds of thousands of people here.

In the elliptical piazza and in the trapezoid-shaped area adjacent to it, chairs have been set up facing the church of St. Peter. People are sitting; many are standing. There is a buzz of nervous anticipation in the air. The crowd is waiting, waiting to see if this afternoon a white cloud of smoke will finally ascend over the church. There had been a black cloud this morning, and the crowd had left disappointed. Some had not left but remained in their seats, not wanting to lose their place, hoping to see the white cloud later in the day. Such is the case of a woman who has eagerly arrived early in the morning with a book in her hand to kill time as she waited.

At around 3:00 p.m., it happens. White smoke. Wild cheering and dancing, shouts of "Habemus papam (We have a pope)!" Now there is a forty-five-minute wait before the newly elected pontiff will appear on the balcony of St. Peter's and say a few words. He finally arrives to a chorus of singing and chanting. Everyone is ecstatic.

But not the woman with the book. She is silently shaking her head. There is a tear in her eye. She is not partaking in the celebration. When the crowd finally breaks up, another woman with a pad of paper in her hand—an American—approaches her. Here is what follows:

Woman with the pad: "I was standing a few rows from you and could see you shaking your head. You don't look happy."

Woman with the book: "I'm not."

"Why?"

"I don't think this is the right person to lead the church now. We could have done better."

"What do you mean?"

"I'm from Boston. You know what's happened there with the abuse. It's where this evil first came to light. This new pope is part of an old system that needs to change. We need someone new, someone who is more of an outsider. This is a mistake."

"What's your name?

"Eileen."

"Can I quote you? Can I use your name in a story I'm writing? I'm a reporter."

"From where?

"The *New York Times.*"

"I . . . I don't know. I'm active in my church back home. My daughter is getting married there next month. I don't want to cause problems."

"I understand. Normally I'd want your first and last name to print a quote. Have a nice day."

The reporter smiles and leaves, and so does the woman with the book. She walks fifteen minutes to the Piazza Navona, where her husband is having a drink. She explains what happened with the reporter and is critical of herself. Her voice quivers a bit. "I should have given her my name. I think it's important for people to have the courage to speak out on this. I blew it."

The couple flies back to the US the next day. When they land, the husband buys a copy of the *New York Times* at the airport. On the front page is an article about the election of the new pope. It reads:

> *The reactions from the crowd in the first few minutes after Pope Benedict appeared on the balcony overlooking St. Peter's Square suggested the division he will have to confront.*
>
> *"As soon as I heard the name, I had a letdown sinking feeling that this man is not going to be good for the church," said Eileen, a Catholic from Boston. She said she was afraid to give her last name because she did not want to cause any problems for her priest and her daughter's upcoming church wedding.*[3]

The husband (me) excitedly shows this to his wife. She breaks out in a big smile, happy that her voice has indeed been heard after all.

Eileen from Boston had done something she felt very deeply about in front of the obelisk that sunny day. I bought five copies of the paper.

The obelisk in St. Peter's Square, where an unknown pharaoh, a mad Roman emperor (Caligula), and modern popes share the stage

The Obelisk at St. John Lateran

Historical Background

The Unfinished Obelisk of Hatshepsut that lies embedded in the quarry of Aswan is the tallest Egyptian monolith in the world. As originally conceived, it would have stood 137 feet and weighed 1,168 tons. It is horizontal, however. The tallest vertical Egyptian obelisk is in front of the church of St. John Lateran (San Giovanni in Laterano). It stands 83 feet and weighs in at 455 tons.

Its journey there is by now a familiar one. It was created by a mighty pharaoh (in the reign of Thutmose III in 1479 to 1425 BCE) and shipped to Karnak. Later a powerful Roman emperor (Constantine the Great, around 340 CE), having made Christianity the official religion of the empire, decided to ship this obelisk to his new capital city of Constantinople, probably as a symbol of Christianity's triumph over paganism. He died before he could move it, but his son Constantius II did so in 357 CE, placing it not in Constantinople but in Rome, in the Circus Maximus, as a companion to the one Augustus had already raised there (the Flaminio). Over time, the monolith fell and broke into three pieces. In 1587 Sixtus V, the "obelisk pope," put a cross on top of it and raised it on a new pedestal with four lions, in front of the church where it still stands today.

This church is officially a Vatican property and as such has extraterritorial rights. In World War II, Pope Pius XII sheltered Jews there, for which he has been honored at Yad Vashem.

It was the last Egyptian obelisk ever shipped to Rome and the only one shipped there by a Christian emperor.[4]

Impressions and Context

I left St. Peter's Square, taking the Metro from there to the Laterano stop. I wanted to see the two obelisks that stand in front of the two most important churches in Catholicism back-to-back to compare them. Although nothing can match St. Peter's in history and setting, the Laterano monument has much to recommend it. The church it fronts is a key one in Catholicism, since it, not St. Peter's, is the official seat of the pope as the bishop of Rome. The popes used to live here before the papacy was moved to Avignon, France, in 1309. When the papacy returned to Rome in 1376, they took up residence at the Vatican. Nevertheless, St. John Lateran still has a lot of cachet. Besides being the ecumenical church of the Catholic faithful worldwide, it is the oldest church in Rome, dating back to 324, and it is the oldest basilica in the Western world. The square in front of it has little of the grandeur of St. Peter's. It is a little stark and windswept. With the tallest standing Egyptian monolith in the world looming almost defiantly in front of the church with the highest status in all of Catholicism, the two structures convey the feeling of two great rivals that have made a grudging peace with one another.

I spent some time poking around inside the church. The structure and exterior were largely rebuilt by Pope Sixtus V in the late sixteenth century in his ongoing effort to add greater Christian majesty to the entire city. Many fine interior elements were added by Borromini a century later. Eventually I crossed the street and entered the building that houses the Scala Sancta, or Holy Steps. These are supposedly the steps Jesus walked up to Pilate's praetorium in Jerusalem during his passion, and they were brought here by Constantine's mother, St. Helen, in the fourth century. Pilgrims to Rome have crawled up these twenty-eight marble steps on hands and knees for centuries ever since, to reach the former papal chapel at the top called the "Sancta Sanctorum" (or "Holy of Holies").

St. John Lateran is one of the so-called seven pilgrim churches of Rome. In order to further popularize the concept of pilgrimage, St. Philip Neri, in 1553, had the idea of establishing a route within Rome consisting of the four major basilicas of the city and three minor ones. Pilgrims from all over Europe would make their way to Rome and walk the seven-church circuit, sharing a common religious experience through discovering the heritage of the early saints. One of the high points of the pilgrimage was to crawl up the steps to the Sancta Sanctorum. On the day I was there, there was a steady stream of pilgrims, many old and infirm, struggling their way up the stairs.

After a few minutes, I exited and crossed the square to observe the obelisk from another angle. There I saw a sign that said the following:

> *The obelisk of San Giovanni in Laterano is the tallest in the city. From Thebes to Rome, centuries later it was found divided into three parts in the Circo Massimo and was placed here by Pope Sixtus V according to a new road program that placed the obelisks connecting San Pietro and San Giovanni passing through Via Sistina and Piazza Santa Maria Maggiore.*

In other words, the obelisks were wayfinders—points of reference—to help pilgrims move from church to church on their journey. In the process, the pilgrims would pray, meditate, think, and draw inspiration from visiting the most famous churches of Christian antiquity. Physically being in these historic places was the key. It was a way to experience the past and the days when the saints walked the earth.

It was becoming clear to me that these obelisks were providing the exact same function for me—a network of wayfinders that were leading me somewhere, both physically and mentally. I thought (and not for the first time) that I had a lot in common with these ancient pilgrims.

There was one difference, though. They knew exactly where they were going and what they believed in, whereas I did not.

* * *

By now I'd overdosed a bit on religious might and power. The day had been filled with seeing the biggest this, or the oldest that, the most important this, the most historic that. I yearned for something more low-key. So I left the square determined to spend the rest of the day in what was now my typically oxymoronic style—this time as a "pilgrim boulevardier."

In Boston we say there is a Dunkin' Donuts on every street corner. In Rome you could say the same for Catholic churches. Some are historic; some have no real history at all. Some have relics of famous saints; some have a body part of someone who is all but unknown. Some are the venues for concerts; others are quiet as a tomb. Some have some work of great art, like a Caravaggio or a Titian. Most have totally unknown works by little-remembered artists who spent a year or two of their lives creating a statue or painting now hidden in some ignored dark corner. I spent that afternoon and early evening walking the streets, randomly popping into examples of all of the above.

I've done this before. In fact, I do it quite often when I'm in Rome. I have a few favorite churches I make sure I pop into whenever I'm in town, but mostly it's about discovery and serendipity. Along the way, I'll occasionally stop, have a panini or a little vino, and move on. I'll make sure I chat a bit with some of the locals about this or that, more to practice my Italian than anything else. And I'll invariably walk into one or two during a service or where an organist is practicing a piece for an upcoming mass.

That afternoon I made maybe a dozen such church stops. None were for more than ten minutes. In each one I did nothing more than sit there. I can't even say I did much thinking. All I did was take in the experience. Most of the churches were nearly empty.

A high point for me was the wonderful old church of Santa Sabina, high atop the Aventino, one of the seven hills of Rome and my favorite neighborhood in the city. The church sits there quietly, an ancient structure going back to the fifth century. One of the reasons I like it is that in the 1500s, it was totally renovated by the ubiquitous Pope Sixtus V, adding what for him was much-needed Christian panache to a too-simple structure. But in the early 1900s, something interesting happened. The bells and whistles that Sixtus had added were stripped out in an effort to return the space to its earlier, humbler look. There is not a painting in the place, and the overall effect is terrific.

This is a Dominican church and a favorite of St. Dominic himself. He would interrupt his peripatetic preaching to come here and pray when visiting Rome in the thirteenth century. In fact, he lived for a time in what is now the convent next door (St. Thomas Aquinas did too). Inside Santa Sabina is information that explains the Dominican motto, which is derived from the writings of Aquinas. It is "Contemplare et contemplata aliis tradere," or "transmit to others what has been experienced in contemplation." I think this is a fine objective and one that I now realized I'd been trying to attain throughout my wanderings. But I was finding that it's easier said than done. One could even say it's impossible, that words will never suffice. Moreover, if you try to impactfully transmit what you've experienced but are only partially successful, you run the risk of lessening the experience as a result. But we try anyway.

It's one of the advantages obelisks have. They communicate, but not through words. Yes, there are hieroglyph inscriptions on many, and some are of interest from a purely historical aspect. But on the personal level, the inscriptions are unengaging—rather colorless mechanical expressions of praise to a pharaoh or a god. Instead, the obelisks transmit through their shape, locations, and ever-evolving contexts. This allows the observer to look at these contexts from different angles, searching for personal meaning—a kind of Rorschach test that requires one to look within.

. . .

By the end of the day, I felt that I had captured something of the true essence of what religion means, or should mean. It's about finding some catalyst to ignite something within. Some people find it in ritual. I don't denigrate that. Familiar repetition is very meaningful to many people. It is a central part of most religions. Some find their catalyst in dogma. A belief system lies at the heart of all religion. Some find it in simple faith. A cynic might say that faith is a sort of "get-out-of-jail-free card." If you can't figure something out, but you want to believe it, then just surrender and say you accept it on faith. I don't denigrate this either. I've long come to realize that rational thinking can't explain the deeper meanings of life. For example, people a lot smarter than I say that string theory posits that there are eleven dimensions. My mind can't grasp this. With my hearing and eyesight waxing and waning a bit these days, I can barely grasp the three dimensions I know about, let alone the eight I never heard of.

For me the essence of religion boils down to two things. The first is ethics. If religion doesn't directly promulgate and inspire ethical behavior, it strikes me as unworthy of pursuit. What's kept me from totally abandoning Catholicism in the face of scandal after scandal is a priest I respect telling me that if you lose faith in the clerical hierarchy, go back directly to the source—in this case, the teachings of Christ and their underlying morality. That seems like good advice, not only for a disillusioned Catholic but also for followers of all religions—because, when you strip away all the ritualistic and dogmatic scaffolding that has been added onto them over the centuries, you find that they all have a lot in common at their core regarding ethics and morals.

My afternoon of church wandering also brought home to me the second essential part of religion: a sense of wonder triggered by simple, individual experiences. A church with no service going on, no sermon, maybe even no other people, is the perfect environment to ponder where every object, place, idea, and emotion we know could have originally come from. We cannot grasp it, and it gives you hope that there is something bigger than us and that unites us all at some level. You'll never figure it out rationally, but you can experience it a bit in the process. To me, that's the ultimate religious experience.

There is no way to prove it, but I bet that's what the average Egyptian experienced when he or she looked at an obelisk in front of a temple 3,500 years ago. They didn't think of dogma or the words of a pharaoh. They just saw a frozen ray of sunlight that left them with a sense of wonder.

Chapter 10

ROME: THE OBELISKS OF ART

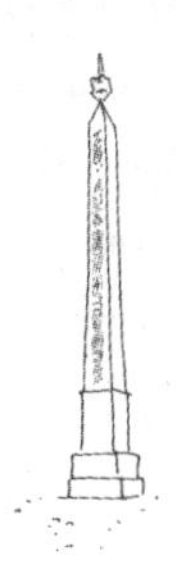

The San Macuteo Obelisk (in the Piazza Della Rotonda)

The Obelisk in the Piazza Della Minerva

Historical Background

The San Macuteo Obelisk (in the Piazza della Rotonda) is twenty feet high and was first raised in Heliopolis as one of a pair during the reign of Ramesses II (1250 BCE). Having been brought to Rome at an unknown time and set up at a shrine devoted to Serapis and Isis, called the Serapeum, it was eventually toppled, buried, and then discovered in 1374 during the reconstruction of the Church of St. Maria Sopra Minerva. It was then raised near the small church of San Macuto, where it became known as the Macuteo, the nickname it still bears. In 1711 Pope Clement XI relocated it to a far more significant location in Piazza della Rotonda, directly in front of the Pantheon. It was placed atop a fountain pedestal that had been constructed 136 years earlier.[1]

The Pantheon is the most perfectly preserved building of the Roman world. Originally built by the general and statesman Marcus Agrippa around 29 BCE, it was almost entirely rebuilt by Emperor Hadrian starting in 116 CE. In 609 it became a Catholic church, which helped preserve it from destruction in subsequent centuries. Today it hosts the graves of a number of important people, including two kings of Italy and several artists, most notably Raphael. It still has a Catholic church within it. Architecturally it has been enormously influential, with many buildings being modeled after its design. To this day, it has the largest unreinforced concrete dome in the world. Its front porch consists of sixteen enormous stone columns, five feet across, and thirty-nine feet high. Each column is therefore almost twice the height of the obelisk they face. Take a guess where these columns come from: the quarries of eastern Egypt.

The obelisk in the Plaza della Minerva is less than two hundred yards away from the Macuteo in the Piazza della Rotunda. It was originally raised in the northern Egyptian city of Sais during the reign of the Pharaoh Apries (590 BCE). We don't know for sure which emperor brought it to Rome (probably Augustus), but it is considered to be one of a pair, its mate now standing in the north central Italian town of Urbino. It originally was erected in the Iseum, eventually fell, and was excavated during the reconstruction of the church of Santa Maria sopra Minerva. This church was built over a shrine that was originally thought to be devoted to the goddess Minerva but is now deemed to be to the Egyptian goddess Isis. This goddess, as I've mentioned, had a significant following in Rome. Several emperors were admirers—possibly even members—of her cult. At least four obelisks currently standing in Italy are thought to have been placed in the Iseum when they first arrived from Egypt, only to later topple, be excavated, and moved to their current locations.

This monolith is very distinctive because of its unique and famous pedestal designed by Bernini, which takes the form of an elephant, trunk swirling across its side, carrying the monolith on its back. It was placed in front of the church of Santa Maria sopra Minerva during the reign of Pope Alexander VII (1655–67), where it stands today. At fifteen feet, it is one of the smallest obelisks in Rome.[2]

Impressions and Context

I stayed in a hotel on the Piazza della Rotonda expressly because of its proximity to both of these obelisks. You walk out the door, and the Macuteo is right there, and sixty seconds away is Bernini's elephant in the Piazza della Minerva. Although it and the Macuteo were not an official pair either in Egypt or Rome, they can be linked together now, first because of their proximity to each other. They are the two monoliths physically closest to each other of all those found in Rome. But beyond proximity, it is interesting to consider these two, so different in appearance and date of creation, as a thematic pair. The message the two of them communicate to us is of the transformative power of art. How do they do this?

First a little review. As mentioned before, Sixtus V can be called the "obelisk pope." At the beginning of his reign in 1565, only one Egyptian obelisk from ancient times had remained standing in the city, namely the one near the Vatican. Sixtus wanted to change that, seeing in these monoliths a way to honor Christ. So he took the biggest obelisks he could find and put them in prominent locations. His first move involved the one already standing in the Vatican. He moved it three hundred yards to stand now in front of the new St. Peter's. He quickly followed that by excavating two monoliths lying in the ruins of the

Iseum. Subsequent popes wanted to erect their own obelisks, but Sixtus had already taken the biggest, most impressive ones. So what was a pope to do?

The answer was to erect smaller ones on tall, impressive pedestals that would add more panache to them. In other words, turn to art. This is exactly what happened with the two obelisks in front of me. The Macuteo sits on top of a fountain on a small hill in front of the Pantheon. The hill, plus the large fountain pedestal on top of it and the obelisk on top of that, conveys a sense of height that this medium-sized monolith does not have by itself. Built in 1575 by Giacomo della Porta and redesigned after the monolith arrived, this pedestal has four dolphins and four lions, each spouting jets of water from their mouths in a kind of pre-Las Vegas style. Frankly, the fountain base is far more impressive than the obelisk. This is one of the things art is supposed to do, I think: take the everyday and familiar and frame it in a way that makes it new and more impactful.

This point is made even clearer with the Minerva obelisk. It is even smaller. What Pope Alexander VII did when he ordered it excavated was pick the rock star sculptor of the day to snazz it up: Lorenzo Bernini. Bernini's track record in obelisk enhancement was second to none. His colonnaded redesign of St. Peter's Square was meant to embrace the Vatican monolith and show it off to its best advantage. And in 1647 he had taken an obelisk of the Roman era whose fragments had been cobbled together in the Piazza Navona and created what may be the greatest pedestal of all time: the spectacular Fountain of the Four Rivers.

Bernini's elephant pedestal of the Minerva obelisk is equally brilliant, if in a much smaller way. Its inspiration possibly comes from a strange 1499 novel called *Hypnerotomachia Poliphili*, by Francesco Colonna, that includes a scene where the main character meets an elephant of stone carrying an obelisk on its back. At any rate, Bernini's whimsical elephant has transformed a rather boring piece of vertical stone into a crowd favorite. It has wit, too, since the elephant's big rear end is pointed at the building behind it, the former headquarters of the Dominican Order. It was the place where Galileo was tried and convicted in true Inquisition fashion. Bernini's advisor on the project was a German Jesuit scholar named Athanasius Kircher, who had no use for the strident Dominicans and would have been pleased with this insult. Or so it is said.

The inscription on the elephant pedestal is the following: "Let any beholder of the carved images of the wisdom of Egypt on the obelisk carried by the elephant, the strongest of beasts, realize that it takes a robust mind to carry solid wisdom."

Although experts are not sure who wrote these words, they don't sound like those of a pharaoh, emperor, or pope, whose inscriptions typically pay homage to a deity, or himself, or both. They sound like those of an artist in support of an idea. It is a call for individual empowerment, not divine intervention.

These two obelisks, taken together, are an illustration of the transformative power of art.

* * *

I poked around both of these piazzas for the rest of the afternoon, and my wandering further buttressed my notion of these obelisks as messengers for the arts.

In the Piazza della Minerva, I was able to spend some time just soaking in the atmosphere of the oldest gothic church in Rome, as well as lingering in front of Michelangelo's statue of the Risen Christ located next to its altar. There are few places in the world where a Michelangelo piece is so accessible.

Then, in the Piazza della Rotonda, I stood in front of the Pantheon. Inside is the tomb of Raphael, Michelangelo's great rival and, some say, the superior painter. The epitaph on his tomb is as follows:

> *If you examine his well-nigh breathing images, you will easily observe the bond between art and nature ... Living, great Nature feared he might outdo Her works and dying, She fears Herself may die with him.*

These words seemed to me a pretty fitting way to end this day, and so I went off for a drink at the rooftop garden of my hotel. From there I could see both of these "obelisks of art," the massive dome of the Pantheon, and the Roman skyline in one panoramic view below.

Rome: the unparalleled city where empire, religion, and art have coexisted for millennia.

The San Macuteo obelisk in front of the Pantheon. Inside is Raphael's tomb with its famous epitaph.

Obelisk atop the famous elephant pedestal in the Piazza della Minerva. Bernini positioned the animal's posterior to point to the left, directly at the former headquarters of the Inquisitors who condemned Galileo.

The Matteiano Obelisk (aka the Celimontana Obelisk)

Historical Background

Standing seventeen feet high, it is the mate of the Macuteo obelisk in the Piazza della Rotonda. They both first stood in Heliopolis and then in the Iseum in Rome, where they eventually fell. This one was found much later, in the thirteenth century, with only the top third intact. To achieve a suitable height, the missing bottom two-thirds was recreated by attaching a four-sided granite shaft to its bottom. It was then re-erected at the Campidoglio (i.e., the Capitoline Hill). When that area was renovated in the 1500s, the obelisk was taken down and lay abandoned for forty years. In 1543 it was gifted by the commune of Rome to Ciriaco Mattei, a member of the nobility and art collector, who then erected it in the garden of the villa he had built on one of the seven hills of Rome, the Caelian. The villa changed hands several times, the last owner being a German. When World War I started, the Italian government seized it because of its German ownership. The garden is now a public park called Villa Celimontana; hence, the obelisk in it is sometimes called the Celimontana. The villa itself is now the headquarters of the Italian Geographical Society.

One grim note. The obelisk was moved to another part of the villa garden in 1817. When it was mounted on its pedestal, the architect in charge was trying to steady it and somehow got his hand trapped underneath it as it was being lowered. The obelisk could not be moved, and the hand had to be amputated. It is still there, between the monolith and the pedestal.[3]

Impressions and pedestal Context

Later that same day, I visited this obelisk, remembering that its owner, Ciriaco Mattei, was one of only three people ever to have an Egyptian obelisk on their private property. One was William Bankes, the polymath we met at Kingston Lacey in Devon. The other was the Medici family member we will meet later in Florence.

I picture Mattei as a dapper elderly man and something of a philanthropist who loves the finer things in life. He has spent much of his life traveling to find art for his collection back at his villa. In that sense, he is a "wealthy vagabondo" (another oxymoron?). I see him as kind and generous too, as it is a well-documented fact that he hosted people from all over Europe who passed by his villa on their way to visit the seven pilgrim churches of Rome. In fact, he was in the habit of throwing picnics for them in his garden, complete with musicians and other entertainers.

His obelisk today is maybe the most out-of-the-way of all the obelisks in Rome. It is located in a nice park, but it is in an area of the city that is little visited by tourists. It is a nice spot for wedding pictures, and I saw several bridal parties there on my visit. Perhaps its only claim to fame is that of all the obelisks in Rome currently standing, this was the first one resurrected when it was raised at the Campidoglio in the 1200s, long before Sixtus V got to work.

On the one hand, it is a reminder of the pleasure of collecting, of surrounding yourself with things you like. Among other things, Mattei also owned Caravaggio's *Supper at Emmaus*. Sounds like it was a rather nice collection, I'd say. But it's also a reminder that someday collections, or actually anything we own, will be no more. We possess things only briefly. Some of our possessions will be bought, some given away, most of them destroyed, because they have value only for the original collector. There is a saying that there are five stages of surrendering possessions: 1) give to family; 2) give to friends; 3) donate to charity; 4) sell in estate or yard sales; 5) call 1-800-Got Junk.

Since I don't own an obelisk or much of anything of great value, I've long been aware that almost all of what I own will end up in the last category. I look at my many rows of my favorite books (almost all paperback) and know they are living on borrowed time. That's a bit sad, but there is a useful message here, and it's one of urgency: to enjoy them as much as we can before they become totally meaningless to the rest of the world. That's what Signor Mattei and his obelisk told me that day on the Caelian Hill.

▪ ▪ ▪

As I've noted, the site of the Celimontana obelisk near Caelian Hill is in a part of Rome I'd never visited before. In my effort to find it, I'd consulted Google Maps on my iPhone that morning. In addition to finding the location of the obelisk, another location popped up called the Palazzo Mattei, about a mile and a half away, back in the center of the city. So after seeing the Celimontana, I decided to walk to the Palazzo and see if I could learn more about the man who had owned it.

I thought I'd try to enter the building, look around a bit, and see if I could get a feel for Mattei the man. I went to the reception desk and explained my purpose. The receptionist referred me to another office up the stairs. When I got there, I saw an unmarked, locked door with a buzzer, which I pressed. A female voice over a speaker said that entering the building was not permitted. I asked if I could at least talk to someone in person to explain. A minute later the door opened, and a husky, bald Italian man stood there behind a gate, arms folded. I judged him to more or less be the place's bouncer (I love the Italian word for bouncer, which is "buttafuori," which literally means "throw out"). He also had more than a passing resemblance to Mastro Lindo, the Italian version of the Mr. Clean brand.

"I'm writing a book, and the Mattei family is in it," I said in Italian. "Can I come in for just sixty seconds and take a quick look?"

"No," he responded brusquely, and began closing the door.

"Is the Center a joint effort between Italy and the US?" I doggedly pursued. "Are there any Americans here I could explain this to? My Italian is not so good."

"No Americans work here. This is 100 percent an Italian institute. Leave at once." He then basically slammed the door in my face.

I don't know what the Italian Center for American Studies is. I have no doubt it is a fine and respected organization. And I guess I can't blame them for refusing to admit a total stranger out of the blue. Still, if their avowed purpose is to promote understanding between Italy and the US, it failed miserably in my case. At a minimum, the Italian Center for American Studies had a chance to study a real American—me—and they turned it down. I have a hunch Signore Mattei would have let me in if he were still around. After all, he was a gracious host to many pilgrims from all over Europe who came unannounced past his villa on their journey to see the seven churches. I was a pilgrim too and can't imagine he wouldn't have given me sixty seconds. He might have even thrown me a picnic.[4]

■ ■ ■

As I exited the building, I crossed the street and quite by accident happened to see a plaque affixed to the wall that gave me pause. It was in commemoration of the most famous act of terrorism in recent Italian history. It was here in this spot, in 1978, that the body of Prime Minister Aldo Moro was found in the trunk of a car. He had been kidnapped fifty-four days earlier by the far-Left group the Red Brigades, who had then assassinated him.

Italy—particularly Rome—has had a heightened awareness of terrorism ever since. For years after the assassination, it was commonplace to see carabinieri with machine guns patrolling Fiumicino airport. They are still a very visible presence around some government buildings and even in some highly trafficked tourist spots, some occasionally standing next to army tanks in times of heightened tensions. Rome is a relatively safe city, but there's still a bit more vigilance that you don't see in other European cities. As I stood by that plaque, I was reminded that I too had been close to two terrorist attacks, and in places you would never expect it.

The first was in Oslo in 2011. Eileen and I were visiting there, just walking around and seeing the sights one afternoon. It was a gorgeous July day in this beautiful city on the Oslofjord. Suddenly we heard an enormous sound and literally felt the earth shake. We had no idea what it was. Some gas pipe must have exploded, we heard someone say in English. For three minutes, time seemed to stand still, no one knowing what to do or what to make of the explosion. Suddenly people began to scatter quickly. My mobile phone rang. It was my daughter in Washington, DC, saying she was watching CNN and a Norwegian official said a car bomb had killed some people near the parliament building and we should get to safety. Later that night we learned that eight people had died in the explosion. Even worse, the terrorist had escaped and gone to a nearby island, where he shot and killed seventy-seven teenagers at a summer camp. We later determined that we had been only one hundred yards from the car bomb. The terrorist, an anti-immigration fascist, remains in jail, defiantly unrepentant.

Then two years later, in April of 2013, Eileen and I had attended the traditional Red Sox Boston Marathon morning baseball game. Afterward we had walked from Fenway Park down Boylston Street, toward the finish line of the marathon. Some of the runners were still coming in, huge, festive crowds lining the street shouting their support. Marathon Monday is one of the best days of the year in Boston.

Suddenly, as we reached the corner of Gloucester and Boylston Streets, there was an explosion. The ground shook. Puzzled looks from everyone. No sign of panic, just confusion. We immediately knew what it was, as it resembled the Oslo explosion. Then a second explosion. Word spread that people had died. Then real fear began to spread, pushing started, and we walked away as fast as we could. The marathon bombing perpetrated by the Tsarnaev brothers had occurred right in our hometown. We had been 170 yards away from the second explosion.

I thought back to Hatshepsut's funerary shrine in Luxor and how it had been the site of the 1997 terrorist attack that had destroyed Egyptian tourism for years. We tend to think that some countries are perpetually on the verge of attack, and we become reluctant to visit them. But the two closest scrapes with terrorism I have ever had were in Oslo, the tranquil home of the Nobel Peace Prize, and Boston, my hometown.

I have long since concluded that bad actors can strike anywhere and that except in extreme cases, I will not be intimidated from travel by world events. I backed off a visit to Damascus for similar reasons long before the real troubles set in there. Now the city will be off limits for the rest of my life. It is my single biggest travel regret. I now subscribe to a piece of advice attributed to Mark Twain:

> *Twenty years from now you will be more disappointed by the things you didn't do than by the ones you did. So throw off the bowlines. Sail away from the safe harbor. Catch the trade winds in your sales. Explore. Discover. Dream.*[5]

Exactly.

If I were younger, perhaps I'd be more cautious. But at my age, excepting an active war zone, there isn't a place on earth that I wouldn't go if it really interested me. I figure at this point I'm playing with house money anyway. And if I have twenty more years left from which to look back, I'll be ecstatic. But frankly, I'm not counting on it.

* * *

I'd now seen all eight Egyptian obelisks of Rome. But I had one more stop to make that evening. From the Villa Mattei I walked a good hour in order to reach the most massive tribute to ancient Egypt to be found in all of Europe: the Pyramid of Gaius Cestius, which was built in 12 BCE as a tomb for a Roman magistrate. It is huge, measuring 125 feet high and 100 feet square at its base. You can't go in it. You just see it from the outside as you drive around it as you enter Rome from the south. It is an impressive sight and makes you realize again how much the Romans were enamored with Egypt.

But I wanted to come to this part of town not to see the Pyramid but rather because it is near one of my favorite spots, the place where I wanted to end my stay in Rome. It is the Protestant cemetery. Here many Europeans, many of them English, were buried in the heyday of the Grand Tour in the nineteenth century. Here are two tombstones that I wanted to be my last memory of the Roman segment of my odyssey. The first was the grave of Shelley, who drowned off the coast of Italy when he was twenty-nine years old. I wanted to pay tribute to the poet who gave us "Ozymandias," with its meaning that was becoming increasingly relevant with every obelisk I saw.

And next to him is the grave of his friend John Keats, who died in Rome of illness at the age of twenty-six. He had little success as a poet in his short life, was largely unknown, and felt he would be soon forgotten altogether. Here is his famous epitaph, which he wrote himself:

Here lies one whose name was writ in water.

It's a message of personal despair. But it's one of universal hope, too, because Keats was wrong. He became famous after his death. His name might not live forever, but then again it just might because of his great art. So while so much of ancient Egypt speaks to the passage of time, Keats and his art represent a kind of eternity, a surprising life after death, a second act—just like an obelisk that has fallen and lies buried and left for dead, only to be resurrected centuries later to speak to a new audience.

It is a message of rebirth, of resurrection, and brings a bit of hope for the rest of us.

Chapter 11

FLORENCE AND URBINO: ON THE ROAD AGAIN

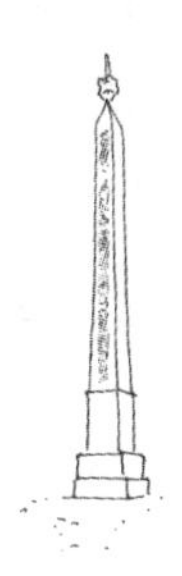

The Obelisk in Florence's Boboli Gardens

Historical Background

It was raised during the reign of Ramesses II (1250 BCE) in Heliopolis, probably as a pair with the Dogali monolith. It was then moved by either the Emperor Domitian or Claudius to the Iseum, where it stayed until 1587, when Cardinal Ferdinando de' Medici bought it and erected it in front of the Villa Medici in Rome. In 1790 the Count of Lorraine, who had married into the Medici family, moved it to Florence and erected it in the Boboli Gardens behind the Pitti Palace. It is situated in the middle of a well-manicured amphitheater-like hippodrome.

The Pitti Palace has a long, proud history. It was originally built by the Florentine banker Luca Pitti in 1458 as his town residence, but he died before it was completed. In 1549 the Medici bought it, and it became the chief residence of the ruling family of the Grand Duchy of Tuscany from 1569 to 1801. The Medici began a vast art collection there. In the eighteenth century, Napoleon used it as a headquarters for his Italian campaigns. In 1870, after the unification of Italy, it was used as the royal palace of the House of Savoy. And finally in 1919 King Victor Emmanuel III gave it to the Italian people. It is now a renowned art museum.[1]

Impressions and Context

Up to this point in my odyssey, I had seen eight obelisks in Italy, all in Rome, all walkable one to the other. To see the last two in the country, I would need to do some traveling. From Rome, the Boboli obelisk in Florence is 170 miles away, the one in Urbino 110 miles further on. While I had enjoyed these last few vagabond days in Rome, I was OK with the logistics change coming up. It would mean I would have to return to the enjoyable road-trip mode we'd had in Egypt.

Moreover, since I'd need to become more mobile and rent a car, I'd be able to work in a few stops along the way, and I had a firm purpose in doing so. This little whimsical project was highly dependent on putting the obelisks in a wider context, most specifically the ancient (Egypt) compared to the contemporary (New York, Paris, London, modern Rome). Another interesting context, though, was the very ancient (Egypt) compared to the slightly less ancient (the Roman Empire). The latter context afforded the opportunity to see ideas evolve, which was a key concept I'd become interested in. So this is what I resolved to do with these final two stops in Italy: to benchmark Egypt versus another old civilization. I'd done this with Stonehenge when I decided to stop there on my way to the Kingston Lacy obelisk, and I thought it had brought a new dimension to my project. For this reason, and because the geography suggested it, I decided to bring the Etruscans into the story.

From Rome to Florence

The Etruscans are an interesting people. They date back to 1000 BCE, with DNA tests suggesting that they originally came from the area of Anatolia, then known as Lydia. This would make them natives in that part of Italy far before the Romans and Latins had arrived. They had no central government or king but rather were a collection of independent city-states that formed alliances among themselves. When the last Etruscan town was subsumed into the Roman Republic in the first century BCE, it marked the end of a distinct civilization that had existed for a thousand years. But despite their great longevity, they remain a mysterious people that we don't know much about. This is because, surprisingly, their language has never adequately been translated to this day.[2]

There are some ancient languages that are totally untranslated, such as the Minoan in ancient Crete. We do know something about Etruscan, because its alphabet has similarities to Greek and some of the words are known. But we don't really understand what the words mean when you put them together. Alone of all European civilizations, Etruscan has no relationship to any language that came before it (it has no Indo-European roots) and none that came after it, because it died off completely when the Etruscans adopted Latin when they were conquered. Much of what we know about them comes not from them but from what others, like the Romans, said about them. These observations are few and far between and probably prejudiced, seeing as the two peoples grew to be bitter enemies. Bottom line: the Etruscans left no Rosetta Stone, nor has a Jean-François Champollion emerged to fully decode the stray inscriptions they left behind.

I planned to make three Etruscan stops before Florence and one after. None would be very long, just enough to get an impression if I could. The first stop was Veii, which had once been the greatest Etruscan city ever before it fell to the Romans in 396 BCE.

There is very little left of the site of Veii itself, just some stone foundations. Excavation is ongoing, and anything that is found of real value goes to museums like the Etruscan Museum in Rome (called the Villa Giulia.) The main impression the site itself leaves is one of ruin, peace, and escape from city life. Yet the fact remains that as the southernmost city in all of Etruria, Veii is located only ten miles north of Rome. The bitterest of enemies, the two powerhouses of their day were almost unimaginably close. Imagine Athens and Sparta being in such geographic proximity.

Despite its meager Etruscan remains, I had one other reason to stop here, if for only an hour. The reason: I had once lived in Veii. When we had moved to Rome in the early 90s for my job, we wanted to live near the American School of Rome, which is out a bit on the Via Cassia. The community of Olgiata was out that way, and so we rented there. It is a fine place, favored by ex-pats, a gated community with much greenery. It is also the site of ancient Veii. We now live in a town south of Boston that goes back to Pilgrim times and was first settled by passengers on the Mayflower in 1627. People here talk about how interesting it is to live in a town four hundred years old. Four hundred years old! As if that were something. I say to people in town, that's nothing. I tell them we lived in a town 2,500 years older that was called Veii. Talk about perspective.

This is a place I think of more and more often as the years go by. There is the historical Olgiata: of the Etruscans, then the Romans, then the hunting grounds of the Papal States. Outside one of the gates is the path where St. Ignatius of Loyola walked when he had a vision that inspired him to create the Jesuits. Go out another, and you walk on the road that the Germans marched down into Rome from their nearby camp in World War II. But more importantly, there is the personal Olgiata: where one daughter learned to ride her bike (the sweating father running alongside in the sweltering heat), where another (the youngest) watched too much Italian TV and began speaking some strange combination of English and Italian ("Aiuto!"), where the ex-pat neighbor from New Jersey could never quite pronounce the town of Civitavecchia ("cheeta veeta vechia" was as close as he ever got), where the American kids went trick-or-treating ("dolce e scherzetto") and approached the house of former LA Laker star and Celtic nemesis Michael Cooper with the fathers chanting, "Coop! Coop! Coop!" (as did fans in the Inglewood Forum in Los Angeles). On and on and on . . . Golden days. Olgiata!

I eventually dragged myself into the present and began motoring toward the coast. The traffic is very light here, and the coastal road offers fine views of the sea. My next stop was Cerveteri, an hour away, and after that, Tarquinia, which is forty-five minutes further on. These two towns and the area immediately around them are where much of what we know of the Etruscans comes from. It is where these people, who had a language we do not understand, speak to us. It is the place where they most come to life. This is ironic, because both are graveyards.

The Cerveteri necropolis is called Banditaccia and has its graves organized in a city-like plan with streets, squares, and neighborhoods. Some of the graves date back to the ninth century BCE. Some are trenches cut into rock; some are tumuli with multiple graves; some, also cut in rock, look like houses with rather detailed construction. For historians, Banditaccia is far more than a cemetery. It is the best example anywhere of Etruscan architecture and what their towns might have looked like.

Tarquinia's necropolis is called Monterozzi and is bigger than Cerveteri, with six thousand graves. The place is best known for wall paintings that are found in two hundred or so of them. Some are very faded, but a few still hold their vibrant color. One shows a banquet, another a wedding. Some show lovers in various forms of what we will politely call romantic activity (the Etruscans seemed to have been very earthy people). A man is chasing a woman he will never catch, both frozen in time forever. The wall paintings of Monterozzi provide us the best direct example of the daily lives of the Etruscans. Again it is a poet, this time Keats in "Ode on a Grecian Urn," who says it best. In the poem, he calls his urn, which depicts similar scenes, a kind of "Sylvan historian" that

Canst thus express
A flowery tale more sweetly than our rhyme[3]

They say a picture is worth a thousand words. This has never been more true than with the Etruscans, because their words mean nothing to us at all. As UNESCO says of Cerveteri and Tarquinia: "Together they represent the sole important attestation of this population that produced the first urban culture in the Western Mediterranean."[4]

As I drove on toward Florence, I thought that I had accomplished what I had set out to do with these three stops. I had been able to provide a good bit of perspective and context that allowed me to compare the Egyptians with another ancient people. I want to be fair to the Etruscans. We may never fully understand their civilization and its accomplishments. We do know that they seemed to have influenced the Romans in terms of architecture (i.e., temple design), sports (such as gladiatorial combat), and religious ritual. But that may say as much about the primitiveness of the Romans in that era as anything else. In any case, neither the Etruscans nor the Roman civilizations of that early era (800–300 BCE) could hold a candle to what the Egyptians had done thousands of years before. If you walk through the dark, cramped Etruscan tombs and then those of the Egyptians in the Valley of the Kings and Queens and see the staggeringly vibrant colors on its wall paintings, its artifacts of gold, the preserved, mummified bodies, some still with facial expressions, you can't help but be struck by the difference. One is a civilization totally dead and mute. The other, though far, far older, feels alive and is very vocal.

■ ■ ■

With this little interlude behind me, I arrived in Florence at the Pitti Palace the next day. I'd been to the palace before to tour its extensive art collections. This time, though, I made for the Boboli Gardens in the back where the obelisk is located. It stands in the middle of an amphitheater, the center of the lower part of the gardens. Before it is the Pitti Palace; behind it and up a hill a fountain with Neptune, behind that one called the Statue of Abundance. Its location tells the usual Italian obelisk story: 1) of power and wealth, because of its Medici owners, 2) of religion, because a cardinal bought it as a gift to his family, and 3) of art, with the museum directly in front of it. It is also another example of a small obelisk (only eight feet tall) becoming something special due to the priority the richest family of its day put on it as the centerpiece of their lavish garden.

I also couldn't help but think of this monolith within the context of its ownership. It was one of three that had been privately held: this one by the Medicis, the Celimontana of Ciriaco Mattei, and the "Rosetta Stone" obelisk in Devon of William Bankes. I judge Bankes to be by far the worthiest of the three owners. The first two had valued the monoliths as baubles for their collections. With Bankes it had been something more. For him the obelisk represented knowledge which he could use to help crack the hieroglyph code to give voice to an entire people. It seems like a pretty good role for an obelisk to play.

I wrapped up the day by taking a quick four-mile drive from Boboli to my hotel in the town of Fiesole. It has a fine Etruscan museum, and

I spent the afternoon exploring it and the archaeological site next to it. Fiesole is a hilltop village that overlooks all of Florence, providing the single best view of the city. I wanted to stay here for two reasons. First, it was originally an Etruscan town, and I wanted the Etruscan angle to end this trip to Florence. Second, Fiesole is the setting of Boccaccio's *Decameron*, which is a series of one hundred short stories a group of ten fifteenth-century Florentines tell to entertain one another as they escape the plague ravishing the city below them. The *Decameron* is a hoot to read, ribald by some people's standards in the past, but really more like a PG movie today, compared to many TV programs you can see on a streaming app. The book had gotten some mention during the Covid pandemic because of the obvious plague parallel, and I had reread some of the stories as a result. Storytelling is the highest art form, in my opinion. If done well, it is both entertaining and able to communicate life's deepest truths as no other art form can.

This was the perfect place to end this first part of my obelisk road trip. As I looked down on Florence below, I knew I wouldn't be able to see the obelisk from here. But I knew it was out there somewhere, mingling with all the great art of the city, telling its own story, as had all the other obelisks I'd seen thus far. So here I was, watching over it from a place where a group of fifteenth-century people, to take their minds off death, had told themselves stories. And they did it in a village founded by an ancient people who have left behind no words to tell theirs.

The Urbino Obelisk

Historical Background

It was originally erected in Sais in the reign of the Pharaoh Apries (589–570 BCE) and is the companion of the "elephant obelisk" in the Piazza della Minerva. It was brought to Rome, probably by Augustus, where it, like so many others, was placed in the Iseum. It toppled, and its pieces were excavated and given to Cardinal Alessandro Albani, who gifted it to his hometown of Urbino when he became Pope Clement XI in 1737. It was erected in the town center in the Piazza del Rinascimento in front of the Ducal Palace, where it still stands.[5]

Urbino is a town with deep artistic roots. Raphael and Bramante were born there, and the Ducal Palace is the site of one of the greatest museums of Renaissance paintings in the world. The museum, and much of the town's development, is due to the efforts of Federico da Montefeltro, Duke of Urbino. He was a Renaissance-era military commander and one of the greatest patrons of the arts in Italian history.[6]

Impressions and Context

It took me three hours the next day to drive from Florence to Urbino. There were other former Etruscan towns I initially thought of working into my itinerary—fine cities of art such as Arezzo, Orvieto, Cortona, and Perugia. But they were a bit out of my way, and their Etruscan remains paled in comparison to what I had seen the previous two days. Anyhow, I knew I'd see them all again someday.

I had never been to the historic city of Urbino. It's off the beaten path in the foothills of the Apennines in the region of Marche. I found it to be an absolute delight and one of the great Renaissance towns in the country. Federico da Montefeltro is key here and is a fascinating character. After a career as a soldier, he became a humanist, civic leader, and patron of the arts. He built a huge ducal palace that served as the center for a court that included musicians, artists, and scholars of all sorts. Located on a remote, rather impregnable hilltop, the town remained an island of learning and tranquility throughout the often turbulent Renaissance. Many luminaries of the day lived or visited here, including native son Baldassare Castiglione, who used the palace as the setting for his 1507 masterwork *The Book of the Courtier*, which outlines what constitutes the ideal courtier. It was one of the most widely read books of the sixteenth century. I would love to have visited that court for even a day, although I suspect the only possible chance I would have had to get invited would be as a court jester. Note to self: rewatch the Danny Kaye movie *The Court Jester* ("The chalice with the palace has the pellet with the potion. The flagon with the dragon has the brew that is true").[7]

Although the obelisk sits on a high pedestal, the monolith itself is only about ten feet tall, making it one of the shortest. Having been found in fragments, the attempts at restoration over the years are obvious, with two of the sides appearing to be in excellent condition, with clearly discernable hieroglyphs, and the other two sides in a deteriorated condition, with no legible hieroglyphs. Interestingly, the four corners of this monolith are cut in a way that makes the structure slightly octagonal, which is unique among all the obelisks. But its location in front of the Ducal Palace is what strikes you most. The duke could not have imagined that three hundred years after his death, an Egyptian obelisk would have been moved to stand in front of his palace. But I bet he would have welcomed it as yet another source of discussion and inspiration for his court. And I think he would also be pleased that he unknowingly played a key role in artistic preservation during World War II, thanks to a fellow citizen of Urbino named Pasquale Rotondi.

In 1943, with Mussolini's regime growing weak, the Nazis had gained control of much of northern and central Italy, its so-called Gothic Line of Defense cutting across the Italian peninsula not far north of Urbino. The Italians heard the rumors of Hitler's desire to build a massive art collection (i.e., the Führermuseum in Linz, Austria) and worried that many great works of art would be looted and carried off. They also were concerned that works would be destroyed by Allied bombings. So Rotondi, the superintendent of the Artistic and Historic Heritage of Urbino at the time, led a nationwide effort called "Operazione Salvataggio" ("Operation Rescue") to hide as many of the country's artistic treasures as possible. With great difficulty, he secretly orchestrated the movement of thousands of at-risk works from all over northern Italy to the Rocca Ubaldinesca, a fortress built by the duke in the town of Sassocorvaro, about fifteen miles north of Urbino. They remained safely hidden there until Italy was fully liberated in 1945. All told, Rotondi is credited with saving nearly ten thousand works of art from looting or destruction. The Rotondi Prize was established in his honor and is awarded annually to the individual who has done the most on an international level to preserve artistic heritage. Just as the Ducal Palace in Urbino had remained a protected island of artistic pursuit despite the wars that surrounded it during the Renaissance, his fortress in Sassocorvaro had been instrumental in protecting the country's cultural patrimony five hundred years later.[8]

For me, the Urbino obelisk was a fitting place to end the Italian part of my journey. It stands in a town not famous for empire or religion but rather for humanism. Even the pope that brought it here is better known as a patron of the arts than for any doctrinal proclamations or actions. My kind of pontiff. The town also provides a bit of closure for the obelisk hunter in Italy, as its most famous native son, Raphael, was born in a house less than a two-minute walk away from the monolith here; as noted in chapter 10, he is buried in the Pantheon in Rome, where one obelisk stands directly in front of him in Piazza della Rotonda and another one to his side in the Piazza della Minerva. The arc of a life . . . obelisks from womb to tomb. As a bonus, the town can boast two of the most consequential art collectors of all time in the Duke da Montefeltro and his kindred spirit five hundred years later, Pasquale Rotondi. The psyche and objectives of the collector—who is someone who does not create himself but appreciates those who do—had become a source of increasing interest to me by now.

Happily, Urbino also has nice sidewalk cafes, in one of which I ended up for a glass of wine late in the afternoon. Although it was mid-September and really wasn't chilly, I had brought my sweater and had draped it across my shoulders, tied below the neck, channeling my inner Marcello Mastroianni one last time. The scene, at least toward sunset, had a la dolce vita kind of vibe, and it seemed like he ought to be here.

I had now seen all the obelisks in Italy, and it was time to return to Boston. From Urbino, I could have chosen to fly from either Milan or Rome, and I chose Rome. My friend and work colleague Stefano lives there, and I wanted to have dinner with him. He had been in Thailand earlier in my trip, and we'd not been able to connect, but he had just gotten back in time for a final dinner with me. I met him at his apartment in the Testaccio area of town, and we walked the twenty minutes to the Jewish section for dinner. On the way I began to tell him about my obelisk project. We were passing by the Circus Maximus, and I told him that a couple of obelisks were thought to have stood here at one time amid all the chariot races and other athletic games.

"It must have been spectacular to see an event here," I said.

"I'm sure," he said. "But great events still occur here. I can think of one in particular."

"Which one?"

"Ours. The one you and I put together. Remember?"

I sure did. Back in the day when we worked together in Rome, our company sponsored a live TV spectacular broadcast from the Circus Maximus to raise money for drug awareness in Italy. The live-in-person audience had been huge—tens of thousands of people had attended the event. Stefano had dreamt up the whole idea and coordinated everything, and since I headed up the department at the time, I got to sit on the outdoor stage set up in the middle of the Circus.

Various celebrities were there, and I sat between two of the best. On my left was Pele, probably the greatest soccer player of all time. And on my right was the boxer and former middleweight champion of the world, Marvelous Marvin Hagler, whose fights against Tommy "the Hit Man" Hearns were legendary. He had moved to Italy to pursue a movie career and spoke very good Italian. His remarks to the audience were far more articulate than mine, given my sketchy Italian. He was from Boston, and we had a nice time talking about the Red Sox (a.k.a. the "Calzini Rossi" in Italian).

"Great times," said Stefano.

Yes, I thought. They were the best. We didn't know it then, but we were so lucky. We took things for granted. Because we were so young and everything was still in front of us, we thought everything was possible, the good times endlessly repeatable. I never played the Circus Maximus again though. But at least I played it once.

▪ ▪ ▪

My odyssey so far had put me in touch with several famous obelisk owners of past centuries, most specifically Ciriaco Mattei in Rome, the Medici of Florence, and William Bankes in Devon. They were all wealthy, and I was not, but we had something in common: we were all collectors. They collected art, and I collected memories.

Some art survives, but personal memories die with the individual—unless they too become art and are passed down in some way in a book, a painting, or an artifact.

I've just passed along a memory of mine in the last few paragraphs. Perhaps it will outlive me if someday some future generation accidentally finds this book (or some Rosetta Stone-like fragment of it) buried in some tomb or cellar or digital graveyard and someone wonders what a TV spectacular was. If the memory is not passed down, it will die. But that doesn't mean it was not worthwhile. It meant something to someone for a short period of time, and in the grand scheme of things, that's probably all we have a right to expect.

The next day I flew back home. I had only one more obelisk to see, and it was in a place that I suspected would have a few very different things to tell me: Istanbul.

Chapter 12

LEVANT INTERLUDE

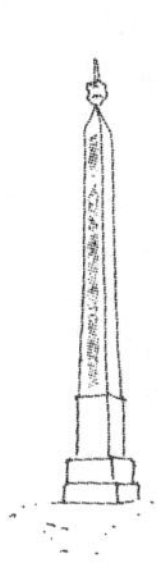

Two days before my flight to Istanbul, I decided on impulse to make a stop first in Lebanon and Israel en route. I did so because I found the idea of doing a bit of wandering intriguing. Most of the journeys I admired most (Ulysses, Herodotus, the medieval explorer from the Maghreb ibn Battuta) had a huge unplanned element to them. Yes, they had an end goal, but along the way, Fate—in the form of a storm or war or an unexpected choice—had always intervened, resulting in an unplanned stop or side trip that invariably produced an interesting result. The essence of an odyssey is serendipity, and although I had some of that in my plan, I wanted a bit more. I liked the idea of tempting Fate into playing a role in my undertaking.

Also, Lebanon and Israel were still on topic for me, because there are some obelisks in both countries. True, they are not Egyptian obelisks and therefore were outside my scope. The one in Israel is a Roman Empire creation of the Hadrian era, and therefore merely pseudo-Egyptian. The one in Lebanon is not only small and in a museum (grounds for immediate exclusion from my hit list) but also not created by Egyptian pharaohs. Instead it was created by a Phoenician king, and therefore technically outside my purpose too. But they were close enough to it to see if they might add any context to my undertaking. Furthermore, I was interested in learning more about the Phoenicians. They were actual contemporaries of the Egyptians. The two peoples were trading partners and in frequent touch with one another. Understanding how the two empires and civilizations compared with one another might be worth my while. That had been the case with the Etruscans and the tribal Britons of the Stonehenge era.

I still had some business connections in the area who would help arrange for guides and drivers to ferry me around—an essential help if traveling alone in that part of the world. So off I went pre-Istanbul for a brief sojourn in the *Levant*, a word now little-used, but one I love because it conjures up images of the retro Baedeker travel era.

LEBANON

Poor Lebanon. Its capital, Beirut, was once called the Paris of the Mideast, but the country has been racked by civil war and government incompetence and corruption for two generations. The period of my visit was particularly unfortunate, because two years previously a huge explosion, due primarily to government negligence, had destroyed much of the port of Beirut. The entire economy was still crippled.

My first stop was the National Museum of Beirut. It is located toward the center of town along what was the front line of fighting in the vicious civil war that destroyed much of the city in the '70s and '80s. Today it is something of an island of stability amid the great uncertainty that characterizes the city and its future. It was virtually empty the day I was there, as significant tourism has yet to return to the city.

It is here in this museum that the Phoenician obelisk stands. A limestone monolith of four feet in height, it was created during the reign of the Phoenician king Abishemu I around 1800 BCE. This makes it the third oldest obelisk in the world (only the ones in Faiyum and Heliopolis in Egypt are older). It is noteworthy for its inscription, which includes the first-ever reference to the so-called Sea People. This is the name now given to a still not entirely understood collection of peoples from various lands in the Mideast who sailed around the area together, sometimes trading, sometimes creating mayhem. The obelisk was found in 1950 in what is called the Temple of the Obelisks in the ruins of the Lebanese town of Byblos.

I spent about two hours in the museum learning more about the Phoenicians. Despite their great antiquity, they are not a total mystery to us, because, unlike the Etruscans, they had a language we understand. It was translated by the French in the 1750s because of its bilingual inscriptions on various stele and sarcophagi, some of which are on display in the museum. The Phoenician alphabet is a big story in and of itself, because it represents what might be considered the first and most important alphabet in the world. Once again, we see the impact of the Egyptians, because this alphabet is based on hieroglyphs. But the Phoenicians made a breakthrough by reducing the infinite variety of hieroglyphs to an alphabet of only twenty-two consonants, which made writing far quicker and easier to understand. The Hebrews, Greeks, Romans, and their subsequent offshoot languages all were greatly influenced by the Phoenician alphabet.

So who were the Phoenicians? The name itself is Greek and refers to a purple dye that was produced in the region and exported around the Mediterranean. The Phoenicians were a seafaring Canaanite people who never thought of themselves as what we would call a "nation." They were a collection of independent city-states along the eastern coast of the Mediterranean, known for their trading throughout the region. One of their largest trading partners was Egypt, which led to the influence each society had on the other.

But the place to go to see and experience what is left of Phoenicia is the coast, not a museum. The entire Lebanese shoreline that fronts the eastern Mediterranean is only 125 miles long, wedged between Syria to the north and Israel to the south. I spent the next two days exploring the southern half of it. Strung along the shore are the once great, now shabby, still fascinating cities of Byblos, Sidon, and Tyre. It is in these three towns that the turmoil of modern-day Lebanon gives way to the past and the mist of time lifts a bit.

But enough. Rather than be a tour guide, it is more in keeping with the spirit of my odyssey to relay an overall impression of the area and follow it with a brief story set in the contemporary world. First the impression.

It is only a seventy-five-mile, 2.5-hour drive along the old Phoenician coast between Byblos to the north of Beirut down to Sidon and then near Tyre, near the Israeli border to the south. This strip is for me like Alexandria. There are so many layers of history that it is dizzying and must be traveled not only physically but in one's head too. First you stop at Byblos, the oldest continuously occupied city on earth, going back to at least 5000 BCE. There you can well imagine the Phoenician ships pushing off, some laden with textiles colored with the purple dye that has lent its name to the region. Others carry the cedar timber cut from the nearby forests of Lebanon that are used throughout the region, including, as legend has it, the construction of the Ark of the Covenant. Some are making their way to Egypt, bearing a substance derived from the cedars that is essential to one of the great achievements of the Egyptians and one that I have not mentioned yet: mummification.

When you get to Tyre, you clearly see (in your mind's eye) the Phoenicians sailing off in the ninth century BCE to establish a colony that will someday become a world power: Carthage, which is in modern-day Tunisia. Hannibal will be born in this colony; St. Augustine will study here and set down thoughts that will prove to be the foundation of much of modern Christianity. And speaking of Christianity, in Tyre and Sidon, you can imagine seeing a person not arriving or departing by ship but on foot. This is Jesus Christ, whom the Gospel of Matthew tells us retreated here from Galilee for a period, marking the only time in his adult life he traveled outside the land of Judaea.

The impression I want to convey is of a small area of unimaginable historic impact that still communicates to us through its geography and setting—where the sea meets the land and the sun is redder than you will ever see when it sets over the water every night.

And now the short story. It is set in Tyre in modern times, because my overall interest is in assessing how the past meets the present. The driver I've hired for the day through my business connections has dropped me off at the entrance to a small archaeological park. A young man wearing a robe and kaffiyeh looks at me with what seems to be surprise.

"Where are you from?" he says in excellent English with a smile.

"US," I say.

"My goodness," he says. "We rarely see Americans here. Welcome!"

"Thank you," I say. I see a lanyard and badge around his neck. "Are you a guide?" I guess.

"Yes. Would you like a tour?"

"Very much."

We spend the rest of the day together. He says he is by trade a history teacher and teaches high school. He is very knowledgeable and engaging. He is so personable that when our tour of the archaeological site is finished, I ask him if he has any time to walk me through some of the town so I can learn more about life here today. He says yes, if I don't mind having his nine-year-old daughter join us. I have no problem with this, at which point a woman with a child approaches us, smiles, and leaves the child with us. The girl is a cute nine-year-old that reminds me of my granddaughter Vivian.

"My wife has an errand to run, and school is over for the day," he says.

We walk through the town.

"How is life here today?" I ask.

"Difficult. The economy is very weak. And there is little tourism because of this." He points to a jeep passing by with two armed soldiers in it. The jeep says *UNIFIL*.

"What's this?" I ask.

"It's part of the UN peacekeeping force here. It stands for *United Nations Interim Force in Lebanon*."

I later learn that this group was put here by the UN in 1978 to end the cross-border conflict between Israel and Lebanon. The border is only ten miles to the south. The UN force has been a presence here ever since, and over three hundred UN troops have died in that period.

We walk through a neighborhood that is orderly but run-down. I see banners hanging from houses with photos of faces on them.

"What are these banners?"

"They are people that have died in the war here. They lived in these houses. We've had many die here over the years. This is my neighborhood. I've known many of them."

We arrive at a small restaurant with outside seating in the shade, and we sit down to order a drink. It is beastly hot and a bit windy. My guide's robe is briefly blown open, and I see he is wearing shorts and a yellow T-shirt underneath. I smile to myself. I had thought it must be unbearably hot to be covered on a day like this, so this attire made sense. Without the robe he'd have looked like a guy from any American city on a ninety-degree day.

We are greeted by the owner, who shakes my guide's hands and hugs the little girl. He places his hand over his heart and says to me, "Welcome."

"This is my friend Hassan," says my guide. "We've been friends our whole lives."

We have our drink and walk around a bit more. We pass by a huge compound composed of a series of crumbling buildings surrounded by fencing.

"What's this?"

"A Palestinian refugee camp. They escaped here in 1948 when they were evicted from their homes across the border in Israel in order to accommodate Jewish settlers. 180,000 refugees fled to Lebanon then, and these camps were thrown together. The people have lived here ever since in tough conditions. Think of it. Families have now lived here for three generations. Seventy-five years they have been here. They are very poor, even poorer than us. They cannot return to their homes. And we are so poor ourselves, we can do very little for them except allow them sanctuary. They are stateless." He spoke in a slow, measured tone.*

Again it was later that I learned that the repatriation to Israel of these refugees with some sort of restitution has been a recurring and unresolved issue in any Israel-Palestinian peace negotiation ever since. Incidentally there are over a million Syrian refugees that have lived recently in Lebanon as well. Since the entire country has a total population of only five million, it means over 20 percent are refugees. This, plus a very small geographic area in which to live, makes the refugee problem in Lebanon among the world's most dire.

It was now late afternoon and time to walk back and meet my driver. We had arranged to meet where he'd dropped me off by the

* I later learned that this was the El-Buss camp, which is one of twelve Palestinian refugee camps in Lebanon. It was originally created in the 1930s for Armenian refugees.

archaeological site in the morning. We passed several more of my guide's friends along the way, and they all greeted him and saluted me. Something seemed familiar in all this, but I couldn't put my finger on it.

Finally we reached my driver, and I shook hands with my guide and thanked him for his hospitality. I patted his daughter on the head and smiled at her.

As I drove away with my driver, he asked me if I'd had any problems. I said none at all. Why?

"Because," he said, "this is Hezbollah territory. Everything's pretty well controlled by the UN here, but sometimes tourists get nervous. They'd rather not come. I was surprised when you said you wanted to."

"I had no idea. I didn't see anything or experience anything where I felt unsafe, thank God."

"Good," said my driver. "You never know. See these two men standing over there wearing the yellow T-shirts? They are Hezbollah."

This startled me. I'd glimpsed my guide wearing such a yellow shirt underneath his robe, and then I realized that several of the friends he'd met had also worn yellow shirts too.

"You know Hezbollah?" asked my driver.

"Only what I've read in the papers. I know most countries classify it as a terrorist organization."

"Yes. The UN considers them terrorist. So do many of the Arab states too. They are Shia and not supported by many of the Sunnis and Christians here in Lebanon either. They now have a paramilitary wing that is stronger than the Lebanese army which they claim is their only protection against Israeli insurgency. They say they have no choice but to be strong or they will be overrun by the Israelis. They also have a political wing that is now a recognized part of the

Lebanese parliament. They represent 10 percent of the parliament now, mostly from around here."

I have thought a lot about this incident ever since. My guide had been friendly, mild mannered, and a good family man and school teacher. He had not tried to proselytize me, had volunteered no opinions, and had merely answered the questions I had asked him. Based solely on my interaction with him that day, you could have seen him as a next-door neighbor.

But the yellow shirt. Was it political? Military? Both? Neither? Did such a distinction matter? Did he condone violence as self-defense? I had no clue. The name Hezbollah means "the party of God," and I will say the name is not a reassuring one. Some will say history shows that the linking of a supreme being to temporal power does not serve the world well. Kings, emperors, pharaohs, and even popes made it a practice in the past, and it didn't always lead to good things. It probably still doesn't today.

▪ ▪ ▪

My next stop was Israel. It is very difficult to get into it from Lebanon. It is impossible to get there directly, because Lebanon does not permit it. This was too bad, because it is only seventy or so miles between Tyre and the obelisk in Caesarea in Israel that I wanted to visit. People walked this entire road as recently as the first half of the twentieth century. But the border is closed now, and so you must go somewhere else first and then transfer to get in.

One of the quickest ways to do this is to fly forty-five minutes from Beirut to Amman, Jordan, and from there take another thirty-minute flight to Tel Aviv. I'd originally thought that I'd use this forced transfer as an opportunity to spend a day or two in Jordan. However I'd already been there a few years previously and had seen the highlights, including the red stone town of Petra. I'd ridden a camel in the desert of Wadi Rum and floated in the Dead Sea. I'd also had a bizarre experience there.

It had been at Mt. Nebo, on the Jordan-Israel border. Legend has it that Moses had stood here and looked out across the valley at the land of Canaan to where he was leading the Israelites on their journey out of Egypt. My work colleague and I had stopped with our guide at a spot where we could overlook the entire valley just as Moses did, a valley he was never allowed to personally enter. It is a quiet, contemplative site, a place where Pope John Paul II had famously once stopped. There is no sign of life below as far as the eye can see.

But on this day we saw, not far from us, a guide with two other tourists. We heard American English being spoken, and we approached them. They were a husband and wife from Scituate, Massachusetts, a town five miles from where I live. We laughed at the coincidence of seeing someone so close to home in such a thoroughly desolate spot. We compared travel stories, and the woman asked why we were there. We told her we were on a consulting assignment, and when we named the well-known US-based company that had hired us, her face immediately contorted into a look of anger, and she quite literally began screaming at us. It seems that the company we named did some animal testing of which she strongly disapproved. We told her we knew nothing of this and couldn't respond. She wouldn't let up, and her screaming echoed throughout the valley. Finally her husband pulled her away. I later learned this company had tested a product under development on mice. It subsequently had discontinued the practice, but not before I had received a tongue lashing as stern as Moses gave the Israelites for worshiping the golden calf.

At any rate, I decided to keep the trip as simple as possible and not stay in Jordan but connect there directly into Israel.

ISRAEL

The historic park of Caesarea Maritima is about an hour's drive north of the Tel Aviv airport. My driver dropped me off at the entrance, where I hired a guide to walk me through.

Caesarea dates back to the days when Judaea was a Roman province. It was founded in 6 CE during the reign of the Romans's handpicked king, Herod. It was probably commissioned to be built by Pontius Pilate, then governor of Judaea. It quickly became a thriving port city for the Romans, complete with a hippodrome. Inside this circus was an obelisk, similar to other hippodromes with obelisks, such as the two of Augustus in the Circus Maximus (now the Flaminio and Lateran obelisks), the one of Emperor Theodosius still in the circus in Istanbul, and the Vatican obelisk that had originally been erected by Caligula in his nearby circus. After extensive earthquake damage, the Caesarea obelisk was completely restored and improved by the emperor Hadrian in 140 CE. It toppled again, was found in fragments in 1995, and was restored and erected here in its original location in 2005.

Like the obelisks in Piazza Navona, the Pincio, and several others of the former Roman emperor, this forty-foot-high granite monolith from the quarries of Aswan is pseudo-Egyptian, commissioned by the Romans and never originally raised in Egypt. It was therefore outside my project. Still I had wanted to see it, as it and the obelisk in Arles, France, were the only two "pseudos" I hadn't seen. Visiting them in situ was something of a secondary objective that I thought might add a bit of a different angle to my reflections.

I actually carried no strong impression away from seeing the Caesarean obelisk and its surroundings. Standing in a remote and little-visited part of the park and only recently erected, it bears no interesting modern history. Nor does it have a particularly unique backstory. I was glad to check the box of having seen it, but was ready to leave after an hour. So I was off to have dinner north of Haifa, and this proved to be more interesting than my site visit.

. . .

It was now early afternoon, and I asked my driver to take me to the Baha'i Gardens at Mount Carmel, just east of Haifa. I'd always wanted to go there, because the Baha'i faith had interested me for some time. It was founded in Iran in the nineteenth century by a Shiite aristocrat named Baha-u-llah who had abandoned Islam to establish his own religion. He was persecuted in Iran for his beliefs and fled the country, living in exile for years and finally dying in 1895 in Acre (Akka in Arabic) just north of Haifa. He is buried there in a shrine to which a steady stream of Baha'i adherents from around the world make pilgrimages.

What had interested me was not any specific dogma or list of beliefs of Baha'i. Rather I find one of its core tenets appealing, which is the essential and equal worth of all religions. I'd grown weary of how all religions have a tendency to separate people by claiming their own individual immutable superiority over all the others. From time immemorial people have believed that there is one path and one path only to whatever they believe salvation is and all other paths are unenlightened. The Baha'i faith seems to be saying something different, that all religions are part of the same religion, just executed differently based on culture and history. I find that intriguing.[1]

The gardens are located at Mount Carmel, which is a small mountain range near the north coast of Israel. The country's largest national park has been created there, and the gardens are within it. They are, in two words, spectacularly gorgeous. They are terraced, with wave upon wave of brilliantly colored flowers winding up a hill that leads to what is called the Shrine of the Bab, a beautiful building where another Iranian, named Ali Muhammad (who came to be known as the Bab), is buried. He founded a religious movement called Babism, which flouted Islamic law in favor of a more individualized form of spirituality. He was viewed as a threat by Iranian authorities and killed by firing squad in Tabriz in 1850. His remains were hidden by his followers for years, and he was ultimately buried in this spot on Mount Carmel in 1909. Baha-u-llah came a few years later and adopted some of Babism's principles. Today Babism and Baha'i are considered the same religion, and the two shrines—Baba-u-llah's in Haifa and the Bab Shrine, with its Baha'i Gardens ten miles away on Mount Carmel—compose the Baha'i World Center.

I had nothing scheduled at the gardens in the way of tours, my intention only being to spend an hour here in private and take in the beauty. The weather was pleasantly moderate, a welcome change from the pressure cooker that was Tyre. As I grow older, I value silence more and more. We are surrounded by constant noise and stimuli. A walk around the meticulously landscaped, tranquil grounds in the late afternoon was all I was looking for.

At some point I noticed a group of six or seven people gathered in a shady spot, engaged in discussion. I approached and guessed that they were Baha'is on a pilgrimage. They saw me, and one of them asked me if I were a pilgrim. I said no, just an interested observer. They invited me to join their circle, and I did.

"Where are you from?" one asked in an accent I couldn't identify.

"Boston," I said. "You?"

"We're from all over—London, Amman, Mumbai, Paris, Denver, Hong Kong." He pointed out the various members of the group. "Are you Baha'i?"

"No. I guess you'd call me a Catholic—sort of."

"Enough said." He smiled. "We've all been 'sort of' something at one time or another. Hindu, Christian, Buddhist. You name it." And he pointed to each member of the group.

The Bahai's do not proselytize, and they respected me as an outsider. When I asked them to sum up what they believe, one said it this way:

"I was born a Sunni in Amman. I believe if I were born in Boston, I'd be a Roman Catholic, and if you were born in Amman, you'd be a Sunni Muslim. It's a matter of chance based on geography and culture. But we all want the same things. We all understand each other on that level, and I believe that's what unites us. We believe in inclusion through diversity. We look for similarities and not differences."

We talked a while longer until it was time for me to go, but as I left there, I said to myself, "That's what I believe too."

▪ ▪ ▪

There was still daylight enough for me to do one more thing before asking my driver to take me to my hotel near the Tel Aviv airport. I told him to drive so I could see a bit of the countryside. He took me north through a beautiful area of rolling hills and green valleys. It reminded me a bit of Vermont. I said as much to the driver, who was a local, well-educated man and also an occasional tour guide himself.

"It's peaceful up here," said the driver. "Until it's not. Remember that Lebanon is only thirty miles across the border from here." And he pointed at the rural, tranquil surroundings.

I thought of the men in the yellow shirts and asked, "Is this where the Palestinians who fled across the border once lived?"

"Yes," he said. "They left in 1948." He explained what I had already learned, that in 1947, the UN voted to create the two states of

Israel and Palestine, and the Jews immediately declared independence. The surrounding Arab states didn't accept it, and war broke out. It was in that period that much of the land here was seized by Israel and the Arabs were expelled. A number of towns around here were totally depopulated, leveled, and repopulated by Jewish settlers. The Arabs fled across the border. They ended up in camps like the one I'd seen in Tyre.

I then asked if Arabs lived here today.

He explained that they do—mainly in the two big cities of the area. About a third of Acre is Arab, but most came in years after the 1948 depopulation. Haifa has a smaller Arab population, but they are among the most prosperous in all of Israel. The locals pride themselves in the relatively good relationships here between Arabs and Jews. It's kind of a model for the rest of the country.

We drove around a bit more, and he showed me some of the depopulated towns. It was a green, fertile land with a quiet peace that felt profoundly fragile. And I thought of Hezbollah and the bleak, crowded refugee camps not far away. Standing there, I could feel in my gut how people on either side of the border would live in constant fear of those on the other side. He then drove me ninety minutes south to my hotel in Tel Aviv.

▪ ▪ ▪

My stop in the Levant had been worthwhile. It had started out as a side trip to see a few minor pseudo-Egyptian obelisks and to learn more about the Phoenicians. I had found the latter particularly interesting. It seemed to me that while the Egyptians had left their obelisks behind to communicate with us, the Phoenicians had left behind an infinitely more flexible mode of communication: their alphabet, which had created a common platform to facilitate communication across cultures. Good. Maybe we can find other common platforms to make communication better and promote understanding. One platform could be binary code (it could prove to be the opposite too). Another could be a faith like the Baha'i that treated all religions equally.

But the stop here had been sobering too. It had developed into more than an exploration of ancient cultures. It had been a startling immersion into two very different contemporary worlds only a few miles apart. This had been one world in a time long ago, originally populated by one people, the Canaanites. But ethnic and religious differences had developed that had turned it into the most complicated place on earth. It was a place where schoolteachers and family men with young daughters were supporters and possibly even members of a terrorist group like Hezbollah.

I knew I had no answers, just one hope: that moderate people of all types raising their children to be equally moderate, would prevail here. Could they find a way, or even want to find a way, to find common ground? Would their leaders do so? Were things moving in that direction in this part of the world? Were they even moving that way back home?

It was my pursuit of the obelisks that had led me to these thoughts. "The world is too much with us," wrote Wordsworth in frustration.[2] I was finding that too on my journey. My pursuit of the obelisks was constantly bringing me into contact with current reality, for better or worse. But wasn't that my purpose to begin with?

It was now on to Istanbul.

Chapter 13

ISTANBUL: TURKISH DELIGHT

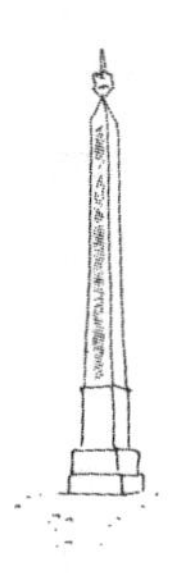

Historical Background

This obelisk was originally created during the reign of Thutmose III to be raised in Luxor at the temple of Karnak. It was shipped there but lay on its side for thirty years. It was finally raised by Thutmose IV around 1420 BCE. Around 357 CE the Roman emperor Constantius II, son of Constantine I, shipped it and a second obelisk from Karnak to Alexandria to commemorate the twentieth anniversary of his reign. Both were among the largest monoliths ever quarried, with a length of ninety-nine feet. The second obelisk immediately went to Rome and was erected in the Circus Maximus (this eventually became the Lateran obelisk). The first one, however, lay on its side in Alexandria until 390 CE, when Roman emperor Theodosius I shipped it to Constantinople, the new city and capital of the eastern empire. Theodosius wanted to continue to make Constantinople a second Rome, and so he raised it in the new city's version of the Circus

Maximus, called the Hippodrome. It was damaged during its relocation to Constantinople and lost a third of its height, and so it stands at sixty-six feet today.

The monolith has hieroglyphs on all four sides that tell of the military victories of Thutmose III. The Romans placed it on a newly created pedestal with various bas reliefs on its sides. Some show Theodosius among his family and court; some show him among his vanquished enemies; one depicts a chariot race. Most interestingly, there is also a depiction of the transportation and the raising of the obelisk. This has given historians one of the best descriptions of the logistical processes the ancients used. It was the last obelisk removed from Egypt during the era of the Roman Empire. The next one would occur centuries later when William Bankes bought the Philae obelisk and moved it to his estate in Devon in 1821.

Two other interesting structures are also situated in the center of the Hippodrome. One is a tall, thin Roman monument erected at some point in late antiquity, probably by Theodosius also. Standing at 105 feet, it was intended as a second and new obelisk to flank the one Theodosius had previously brought from Egypt. This would make the Hippodrome clearly echo the grandeur of the Circus Maximus, which also boasted of two monoliths at the time. This new one was damaged, then repaired in the tenth century by the Roman emperor Constantine VII Porphyrogenesis. Between the two obelisks stands a bronze structure called the Serpentine Column. It was brought here from Delphi in Greece by Constantine I in 324 CE. This twenty-six-foot-high column was part of a sacrificial tripod that commemorates the Greeks who defeated the Persians in 479 BCE in the Battle of Plataea.

The Theodosius obelisk has never been moved or toppled since its arrival in Constantinople in 390 CE. Today the area around the hippodrome is called Sultanahmet Square. It lies directly in front of the famous Blue Mosque which Sultan Ahmet had built in 1609.[1]

Impressions and Context

My odyssey was nearing its end. This would be my final stop, and I was making it with Qaisar Shareef, which was fitting, because he had been there when the odyssey had started in Egypt six months ago. It was also helpful to me because he knows Istanbul like the back of his hand. He went to school in Ankara, speaks Turkish like a Turk, and has many friends in the city, which he visits often. We met up at the airport in DC and flew over together. When we landed in Istanbul, we gathered our bags and exited into the terminal. We were greeted there by his longtime friend Mete, who was going to drive us to our hotel. I swear that the following scene really happened:

The two men embraced, and, after saying a few introductory words in English for my benefit, they began speaking Turkish. After some back slapping and a few laughs, Qaisar turned a bit serious and took one of his pieces of luggage—a rather large duffle bag—and gave it to Mete, who seemed to be extremely grateful and clutched it closely to his side. Qaisar pointed to the bag and made some comment, and Mete nodded. We then walked to Mete's car; he drove into town and dropped us off at our hotel.

A bit later at dinner, Qaisar and I had the following conversation.

Me: "I don't want to be nosy, but what was that you gave Mete at the airport? He seemed really happy."

Qaisar: "You mean the duffel bag?"

Me: "Yes."

Qaisar: "Underwear."

"What?"

"New underwear. You know, jockey shorts, that kind of thing."

"Really?"

"Really."

"Wow. He's this very successful businessman and picks us up in a BMW, and you give him underwear?"

"Yes."

"And I was thinking if I didn't know you better, I'd think this was some sort of drug deal. He was holding it so closely, like some treasure."

"Well it kind of is. It's his favorite brand—Fruit of the Loom. You can't get it here in Turkey these days. So he asked me to bring some over."

Pretty interesting, I thought. The ancient Egyptians supplied the world with obelisks. The US supplies underwear. The global supply chain continues to evolve.

* * *

I stood looking at the Hippodrome, with the obelisk of Theodosius in the center of it. It is one of the most impressive sites of all of those I'd visited. It is certainly one of the most thought provoking. Here converge several recurring threads weaving throughout my odyssey. Actually, *converge* is not the right word. This is a place where different worlds seem to collide.

The first world is that of the ancient Roman Empire. You have to keep reminding yourself that it was an emperor who put this monolith here in the first place as part of an ongoing effort to create a new city in the image of imperial Rome. He succeeded completely. In fact, of all the obelisk locations in the world today, including those in Italy, this one in Istanbul is maybe the best representation we have of the world of that empire. Unlike all eight of its counterparts found in Rome, it was never excavated or moved by any pope. It has never fallen. It is in its originally intended position, one that predates any other obelisk location outside of Egypt. Further, this monolith that Theodosius brought directly from Egypt and the other he created soon thereafter as its mate stand close together in a space that you can still easily picture as a chariot racecourse. The scene gives you a far truer sense of what the Circus Maximus must have been like during the imperial days than the empty, windswept Circus of today.

There are other elements here that conjure up antiquity. The obelisk's pedestal doesn't merely have the usual inscriptions with formulaic platitudes in praise of a god, an emperor, or a pope. It has actual scenes depicted in bas relief on it—of the chariot races, of the emperor's conquests, and astoundingly, of its transportation from Egypt and to this very spot. It is storytelling of the highest order. The Greeks are part of the story too, with the Serpentine Column from Delphi connecting the viewer to a world that existed before there was a Roman Empire.

But then you look up and around, and you see another world. You see the world of the seventeenth-century Ottomans with the minarets of the Blue Mosque of Sultan Ahmed towering nearby. Its minarets have as dramatic an impact on the viewer as do any of the obelisks from Aswan. From several angles the two obelisks in the Hippodrome are visually bracketed by the minarets, dwarfed by them, really. And these minarets have something the obelisks have never had. They have sound. When the call to prayer arrives and the muezzin starts his chanting, the whole scene changes. In those moments, the pharaohs, emperors, and even the sultan step aside and turn the stage over to the words of the prophet and to Allah.

When the call to prayer starts, as it does five times per day, life does not stop on Sultanahmet Square. People still walk, and cars still speed through the streets around it. But the amplified, penetrating sound projecting over the loudspeakers cannot help but call you out of your everyday life, if for only a minute or two. The words uttered in Arabic, although unintelligible to some, still produce an otherworldly effect. The sound itself seems to exhort you to step back, to reassess, to place things in greater perspective.

The greater perspective I had in mind now was of a religious nature. Most of the eleven obelisks of the former Roman Empire standing today have Christian connections. Except for the one gifted to Ciriaco Mattei by the city of Rome, all of the other nine in Italy were moved to their current locations by popes. In doing so, Christianity, in essence, co-opted the pagan religion of the ancient Egyptians and made it subservient to its own.

In Constantinople, a similar thing has happened, but with a far different outcome. The obelisk of the Emperor Theodosius, a Christian himself, was once surrounded by Christian churches on all sides. Over time, those churches have been leveled and replaced by mosques. Now minarets rim the square. In Egypt, you can see obelisks near mosques with minarets. In Italy, you can see obelisks near churches with towering spires. But it is in Istanbul where you see an even more complicated evolution. It is only here in this place that the Sun God Ra was made subservient to the Christian God of the Trinity, and that God in turn was totally displaced by the Allah of Islam. Three different civilizations with three different religions. Actually you could say there is a fourth. It was here that a schism split the Christian Church in two in the eleventh century, and for a thousand years Istanbul was the home of the most influential patriarch in all of Christian Orthodoxy.

While it's easy to see a world of differences here, there is something else too. For many reasons, most of them cultural and not spiritual in nature, these religions have drifted apart, sometimes belligerently. But I see a similarity among them all: the universal need of people to believe in something bigger than themselves. It has been visually expressed in many different ways through the ages, such as minarets on mosques or spires on massive cathedrals. But the underlying need is the same, and it was first addressed by the Egyptians with their obelisks thousands of years before the others.

* * *

Qaisar tells me there is no word in either Turkish or his native Urdu that corresponds to flaneur, so let's just say he and I idly strolled around Istanbul for the next couple of days. While Rome is my favorite city, this is his, each resembling one another in terms of history, atmosphere, and street life. Its setting on the Bosporus and the Golden Horn is hard to beat—a good blend of the bustling present and the evocative past, a true crossroads of the world. Like Rome, it is a city that is a unique mixture of empire (Topkapi Palace, Roman walls), religion (from mosques to dervishes), and la dolce vita Turkish-style (the Grand Bazaar, restaurants along the water front, sidewalk cafes). All of this we saw in those two days.

And then it was time to leave. I'd now seen all the obelisks of the former Roman Empire. They had introduced me to pharaohs, emperors, kings, and popes. They had told tales of empire, religion, and art. Some of their messages were political and governmental, some spiritual, some philosophical, some personal. I wanted time to process it all.

Importantly I wanted to fold these recent trips to Italy and Istanbul into my experiences first in Egypt and then in New York, Paris, London, and Devon. I needed to look at the whole thing, all the obelisks collectively, and I wanted to do it alone. So the next day Qaisar and I shook hands at the airport, he to go to Karachi to visit family, me to drive three hours to a place that might help me collect my thoughts now that my odyssey had ended. And what more appropriate spot to do so than the place where the greatest odyssey of them all had ended: Ithaca.

The obelisk in the old Roman Hippodrome in Istanbul,
now surrounded by the spectacular minarets of nearby mosques

Chapter 14

JOURNEY'S END ON THE WINE-DARK SEA: FINAL THOUGHTS OF A MAN OF LEISURE

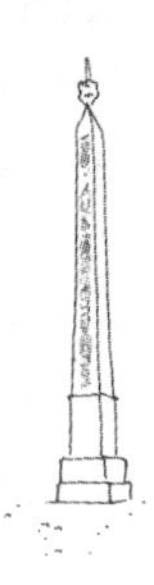

Ending my journey exactly where Ulysses had ended his seemed like a great idea, and I had planned to make this small island off the west coast of Greece my final stop for weeks now. But it was not to be, because a major storm moved into Greece and the western islands. My flight from Istanbul to the island of Cephalonia was cancelled, as was the ferry from there to Ithaca. All alternate flights were sold out for days, and since Ithaca is difficult to get to under the best of circumstances, I was forced to abandon this idea. I had to make a quick decision, and so I chose a place I knew I could get to but that also had some symbolic cache of its own: Troy.

Although I was quite disappointed that my original plan had fallen through, this new one at least had the benefit of working very well logistically. I would not even need to fly—I could easily get there by car from Istanbul. As noted earlier (see chapter 2), I had been to Troy years before, driving from there into Thrace to recreate the first leg of Ulysses's windblown journey into my supposed ancestral homeland, the land of the Cicones. So I rented a car in Istanbul and headed southwest to make the four-hour trip.

On the way down, I stopped at Gallipoli and explored the scene of the notorious World War I battle that made Ataturk famous and almost ruined the career of Winston Churchill. I then crossed over the Dardanelles, the strait that separates Asian Turkey from European Turkey. Others have had trouble making this crossing in the past. In Greek myth, Leander had drowned on one of his nightly swims from one side to the other trying to meet his lover Hero. And in 482 BCE, a tempest had destroyed the pontoon bridges the Persian king Xerxes had built for his army to cross into Greek territory. Herodotus says Xerxes was so enraged that he gave the water three hundred lashes and branded it with red-hot irons as the soldiers shouted at the waves below.[1] But on this day, the weather here was fine for me, and the only shouting that could be heard was from me, windows rolled down, loudly singing songs from my playlist. I took the road that hugged the coast until I reached the area south of the modern town of Çanakkale, which most experts believe is the site of ancient Troy.

The whole scene works for me. Yes, there is what some would call a cheesy wooden Trojan horse replica in town. I think it adds nice, if not necessarily accurate, imagery to the entrance to the archaeological park (remember, I like sound and light shows and Agatha Christie novels). The park itself is a working excavation site with interesting information.

But I was here to collect my thoughts, not sightsee. Could the place where Ulysses started his journey serve as inspiration to help me assess mine? I spent most of my three days here not at the excavation site but walking along the Dardanelles (or to call it by its more prosaic ancient name, the Hellespont). After all, it is water, the wine-dark sea, that is at the heart of Ulysses's journeys, the common thread that runs through all his adventures, just as the Nile underlies all the journeys of the obelisks.

Little by little, I was able to put my journey into perspective. The facts were that I had made four separate trips over the course of seven months to see the obelisks. Although the basic logistics of each trip (flights, hotels) needed careful advanced planning, much of the daily itinerary was extemporaneous. I wanted to relax, to keep the fun with a purpose approach front and center. I had succeeded in this.

What had I gotten out of all this in the final analysis? Anything important? One of the models behind my undertaking was the Camino de Santiago de Compostela, the medieval pilgrimage route across northern Spain that leads to the place where James the Apostle died. Many modern people who make that walk today call it a life-changing experience. Was that the case with me? On my last afternoon there, I sat on the patio of my hotel overlooking the Dardanelles and asked myself that exact question.

I reflected that my odyssey had consistently challenged my thinking in specific areas, namely politics, religion, and art. Did I now think any differently about any of those topics? Probably not. Much of what I had already believed had been reinforced, though, and there is great value in that. On politics, I would remain open-minded on policy but even more fiercely opposed to divisive culture warriors that seek to divide people. On religion, I would be even more motivated to value the original ethical and spiritual underpinnings of a belief system rather than the doctrines and hierarchy that get added in later. With art, I saw no reason to change my preferences (novels—any era; poetry—anything before 1940; music—classic rock and some Italian opera; painting—impressionism; movies—anything between 1935 and 1955, mostly anything foreign). The obelisks had provided a neat framing device for reexamining many assumptions I had built up over the years.

But my biggest "ahas" tended to be—how can I put this?—less topical and more philosophical in nature. It was less about examining specific themes and more about a general reassessment (perhaps an acceptance?) of the human condition—and human nature too. Here's what I mean specifically.

1. **Although a few famous names spring out, almost all of human history is populated by nameless, faceless people.** Every time I saw an obelisk, I thought of the many thousands—millions—of people who worked their lives in total obscurity to create them. For every emperor, pharaoh, king, dictator, or pope, there were the countless people that followed them, fought for them, died for them, on occasion struggled against them. We will never know anything about these people. And so it will be for all but a few of us. Future generations will know absolutely nothing about most of us.

Significantly, I encountered few famous women on this journey. Hatshepsut is a major exception (but even she had to hide her gender). Cleopatra is another. The women did not fight in the wars, build the obelisks, or create any of the art. With the exception of the female goddesses, most of the names of the "real" people we remember of ancient Egypt are men. The women were behind the scenes, and they are totally anonymous. George Eliot gets at this anonymity at the ending to her novel *Middlemarch.* She is referring to her heroine Dorothea Brooke, but I think she is speaking for all of us who achieve no fame: "Her full nature, like that river of which Cyrus broke the strength, spent itself in channels which had no great name on the earth. But the effect of her being on those around her was incalculably effusive: for the growing good of the world is partly dependent on unhistoric acts; and that things are not so ill with you and me as they might have been, is half owing to the numbers who lived faithfully a hidden life, and rest in unvisited tombs."[2]

I saw many spectacular tombs on my journey: the funeral chambers in the Valley of the Kings and Queens in Luxor, the Etruscan necropolises in Cerveteri and Tarquinia, the graves of the recently famous in Père Lachaise in Paris. All interesting. But now that it is all over, what has left the biggest impression on me are not the famous people and the great moments in history I learned about, but rather the millions—billions—of those who have led a hidden life I will never know who rest in tombs neither I nor anyone else will ever visit. It's the story of mankind. It will someday be the story of almost everyone now living—and me. It makes you feel like part of some long gray line, and there is comfort in that.

2. Human nature has not changed over the course of history. The population of every civilization has been tribal. We are so today. People have divided themselves into religious sects, political factions, ethnic enclaves throughout time. The same issues arise again and again. And this leads to a great paradox. Yes, tribalism results in separation, often conflict. Pharaohs, kings, religious figures, and demagogues have all throughout history sought to tap into the exact same emotions to enlist support, passion, and sometimes hatred against other tribes. Modern rulers do the same thing, often intentionally promoting divisiveness for their own benefit. Yet if you look beneath the surface—and here's the paradox—all peoples in all eras throughout history have shown the same basic wants, needs, hopes, and fears. You'd think there would have been a way to find more unity of belief and purpose. But we have not. Each generation appears to need to learn the lessons of history all over again. It will always be so, but will we even put a value on trying to learn from history in the future? The current evidence is not encouraging.

A careful look at the Churchill quote at the front of this book adds, I think, an important insight in this regard. It implies that not only is looking at history relevant for understanding today and tomorrow but that *ancient* history is particularly so. I have come to believe that "the longer we look back," as Churchill puts it, allows us to better identify the ebbs and flows of beliefs and values, of recurring themes, of long-term cause and effect, and the predictable consequences of repeated mistakes. Importantly, looking far into the distant past makes it easier to strip way our current biases and paradigms and to look dispassionately and objectively at the factor that most influences the course of history: the nature of man.

3. This point about human nature brings me to the very crux of what I now believe my odyssey was really about. As I've mentioned, I thought the perfect place to end my journey was the island of Ithaca, where Ulysses ended his. This is where he was trying to get to for ten years. It was home, it was where peace and stability could be found. Reaching it was the desired final outcome, the journey to get there was an unwanted burden. So how does it end for him? He arrives in Ithaca, where he finds his wife is being harassed by suitors, his rule imperiled. He then annihilates all his competitors to the extent that Venus needs to step in and stop him. She does, and his rightful place with his wife and kingdom is assured. Ulysses has triumphed, and he can resume his calm life pre-Trojan War. It is the kind of ending that Homer's audience would have been expecting.[3]

Over the next couple of days, I read and reread that ending several times until one night a thought suddenly struck me. The ending is all wrong, at least for me. I assessed how I felt now at the end of my journey and what I had experienced over these last months, and I realized that an odyssey is not about reaching an endpoint. It is about the effort to get there. Although my journey had now technically ended, I had more questions than answers. The obelisks had expanded my thinking, not narrowed it. I had wanted them to talk to me and explain things, but I found I had talked to them too. We'd had an open-ended discussion on the past, present, and future—my future. I was aware that what had started as a way to kill some time had evolved into a sort of ill-defined personal quest. I had a sense of completion and fulfillment. But I had no sense of closure.

In his poem "Ulysses," Tennyson envisions Ulysses on Ithaca not as a happy man living a life of satisfaction. He is depicted as wasting away, perhaps despondent. He has reached his goal and found it wanting. He regathers his men to start anew on another quest.[4] Some will say this wanderlust is admirable (this was John F. Kennedy's favorite poem). Others will say it is a flaw. Regardless, it is the deepest insight into human nature I know and is my top takeaway from my trip. Reaching an Ithaca—the end—does not provide permanent satisfaction for many of us. The effort, the aspiration to get there, is the best some of us will ever do. I had ended my personal odyssey at the right place, at Troy, where voyages begin.

My journey has highlighted more than ever for me the importance of words. Once men were able to translate hieroglyphs, they understood and could appreciate the Egyptians. Because we don't understand Etruscan words, we do not understand or fully appreciate them as a people. So let's call upon the one who uses words best—the poet—to have the last word. A poet is maybe the only person who can make the point that needs to be made here. I have quoted a number of poets along the way. But they have all been English. Let's end with one from a place that's far more appropriate: Egypt. Constantine Cavafy, from Alexandria, also wrote a poem about Ulysses, called "Ithaca," and he, like Tennyson, nails it. Here is an excerpt:

When you set out on the journey to Ithaca
Pray that the road be long,
Full of adventures, full of knowledge . . .

Always keep Ithaca in your mind.
To arrive there was your final destination
But do not rush the voyage in the least,
Better it last for many years,
And once you're old, cast anchor on the isle,
Rich with all you've gained along the way,
Expecting not that Ithaca will give you wealth.

Ithaca gave you the wondrous voyage:
Without it you'd never have set out.
But she has nothing to offer you any more.

If then you found her poor, Ithaca has not deceived you
As wise you've become, with such experience, by now
You will have come to know what Ithacas really mean.[5]

"Pray that the road be long, full of adventures, full of knowledge. Do not rush the voyage in the least. Better it last for many years." Perfect, I think. At least it's where I'm at. I'm ready to go again, to make a new beginning. And then another and another, as long as I am able to. As if to breathe were to live.

But the years are few, and I have a new sense of urgency. In that spirit—and if you'll permit me one last oxymoron—I'll sign off as "a man of complete but urgent leisure."

Afterword

UNFINISHED BUSINESS

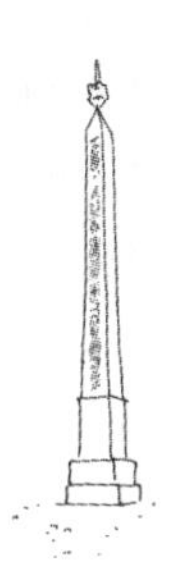

The first priority of my undertaking was to see all fifteen of the Egyptian obelisks that have left the country and are now standing outdoors in public spaces elsewhere. I have done this, and in the preceding chapters I have included some facts regarding them as well as my own impressions of each.*

I want to finish by giving a fuller picture of other famous obelisks. They fall into five classifications: 1) Obelisks still standing in public spaces in Egypt; 2) Ancient Egyptian obelisks in museums; 3) Ancient pseudo-Egyptian obelisks in the former Roman Empire; 4) Ancient pseudo-Egyptian obelisks (all others); 5) Important modern obelisks.

What follows are just the facts.

* Much of the information in this section is based on personal site visits, many with on-site guides. More information was acquired through follow-up research, which is mentioned in the relevant footnotes. Some of the most helpful books on this subject are listed in the Bibliography.

I. OBELISKS STILL STANDING IN PUBLIC SPACES IN EGYPT

Beyond the fifteen that have left Egypt, there are eleven still standing within the country. My secondary goal was to see all of these too. I have not done this yet. I saw the eight that I've noted in chapters 1, 2, and 3, because they just happened to be located in areas that were on our itinerary, whereas the three I have not seen were not. Since I had not formed the idea of my project at that time, I had made no attempt to see them then. While the timing has not worked out for me to see these three yet, having done so would not have changed the overall thrust and perspective of the book. Besides, I am now convinced that the most meaningful odysseys are never really over, and it leaves me with an incentive to return to a country about which I have so much still to learn. In the interest of completeness, here is a list of all eleven. The first eight are the ones I've seen. They are the ones that inspired the entire odyssey.

Of the eleven, six are still in situ in their original location—the three standing at Karnak, the ones at Luxor Temple and Heliopolis, and the Unfinished Obelisk still embedded in the Aswan quarry. The five that have been moved include the Faiyum obelisk (number 9) which was moved there in 1971, the three in Cairo (numbers 6,7, and 8) which were moved to their positions in 1984, 2020, and 2023, and the one in New city El-Alamein moved in 2019.

1. *Unfinished obelisk (in Aswan quarry).* It is unique among all of the twenty-six Egyptian obelisks, because it is the only one not standing. It developed a crack as it was being built and was never carved out of its quarry in Aswan, where it remains embedded today. It measures 138 feet, and had it been erected, it would have easily been the tallest monolith of them all. The tallest currently standing is

at St. John Lateran in Rome, at "only" 105 feet. It was created by the female Pharaoh Hatshepsut (1479–58 BCE). See Chapter I for more context.

2. *At Karnak Temple* (the Thutmose I obelisk). It was raised at the temple dedicated to Amun-Ra during the reign of Thutmose I (1506–1493 BCE). It is only one of six Egyptian obelisks in the world still in situ in its original location (numbers 1, 3, 4, 5, and 10 on this list are the others). It was one of a pair, the fragments of its mate lying nearby. See Chapter 2 for more context.

   It is 64 feet high and weighs 143 tons.
3. *At Karnak Temple*: the obelisk of Hatshepsut (1479–58 BCE). It stands at an entry to the temple of Amun Ra and within 50 yards of the obelisk erected by her father, Thutmose I. It is 83 feet high and weighs 323 tons. Carved on its surface are scenes of Hatshepsut and her stepson Thutmose III offering gifts to Amun-Ra. The pyramidion was covered with a substance called electrum, which would have made it glow in the sunlight. There is an inscription on it in which the pharaoh says she was begotten of Amun and possessed in her soul and body all the qualities of the gods. She says she is the "God of All" in the form of a woman, Amun's counterpart in every way. See Chapter 2: Luxor for more context.
4. *At Karnak Temple*: the obelisk of Seti II (1200–1194 BCE). It is composed of red sandstone, as opposed to the usual red granite from Aswan, which means its surface has deteriorated. Standing in a rear entrance to the Great Temple, it is small and unassuming and often goes unnoticed. See Chapter 2: Luxor for more perspective.

5. *At Luxor Temple.* It was erected in the reign of Ramesses II (1279–13 BCE) as one of a pair that stood at an entrance to the Luxor Temple. This one is the taller of the two at 82 feet. For unknown reasons, its eastern and western sides are slightly convex. It is one of the six Egyptian obelisks still in situ in its original location.

   Luxor Temple was built from Nubian sandstone around 1400 BCE, 150 years before the obelisk arrived. It is not dedicated to a specific deity or pharaoh but rather to the general renewal of kingship. There are four baboon statues around the pedestal, looking at the sun in adoration. Baboons seemed to have been a favored animal in the time of Ramesses II.

   The Luxor Temple was connected to the massive Temple of Karnak by the Avenue of the Sphinxes. This 1.7-mile path was completed in the reign of Nectanebo I (380–362 BCE) and was subsequently buried in sand for centuries. Its path was found in 1949 when a number of statues that lined the original route were discovered. By 2000, the entire pathway was rediscovered and over 1,000 statues now line it. Eight hundred and seven are sphinx-shaped (body of a lion, head of a human), and 250 have a ram-shaped head. Final restoration was completed in 2021, and the walkway lined with many sphinxes is now open to the public. The archaeologist Zahi Hawass has called the Luxor site "the largest open air museum, the largest archaeological site in the world that tells the history of Egypt from the 2000 BCE era known as Dynasty XI—until the Roman Period." See Chapter 2 for more context.

   The original mate of the Luxor obelisk was taken away by the French in the 1830s. At seventy-five feet tall, it now stands in Place de la Concorde in Paris. See Chapter 5 for more context.

6. *In Cairo* (at the Cairo airport). It was originally erected during the reign of Ramesses II (1279–13), probably at his capital city of Pi-Ramesses, and later moved to Tanis. It eventually fell and was in fragments until 1984, when it was repaired and raised at the airport. It stands on a large pedestal in a little park near the main terminal. You cannot enter the park, but the obelisk is clearly visible as you approach the terminal by car or by foot from any of the adjacent hotels.
7. *In Cairo* (at Tahrir Square, erected 2020). It was originally erected in the reign of Ramesses II (1279–13 BCE), found in fragments in San el-Hagar (Tanis), and restored to a height of sixty-two feet and placed on a small hill in the center of the square as part of a major renovation project. Four sphinxes removed from Karnak Temple are also a part of the renovation. It is very difficult to approach the obelisk, as it stands in what is in essence one of the busiest traffic circles in Cairo.
8. *In Cairo*: The Hanging Obelisk (in front of the GEM museum). It was erected during the reign of Ramesses II (1279–13 BCE) in Pi-Ramesses. It was later moved to Tanis, where at some point it fell and lay in two pieces for centuries. In 2021 it was meticulously repaired, cleaned, restored, and erected in the courtyard near the entryway of the new Grand Egyptian Museum (GEM).

   It is referred to as "hanging" because it stands elevated off the ground on a platform, which enables tourists to walk underneath the obelisk, stand on a plate of glass, and look up into its interior. Clearly visible in the interior is a rare cartouche of Ramesses II that has been hidden from sight for 3,500 years. From the base of the monolith, you can see the pyramids in Giza two miles away.

The GEM museum will fully open in 2023 and will house many valuable objects, some that were never displayed before and some that are currently in other museums, such as the golden mask of King Tut.

9. *Faiyum obelisk (a.k.a. Abgig).* It was erected during the reign of Senusret I (1971–26 BCE) in an ancient site called Abgig near the modern town of Faiyum, about a hundred miles southwest of Cairo, in middle Egypt. It has a rounded top and now stands in a traffic circle in Faiyum.
10. *Heliopolis obelisk (a.k.a. al Masalla).* It is the oldest standing Egyptian obelisk in the world. It has been in its current location without falling since it was erected during the reign of Pharaoh Senusret I (1971–26 BCE). At one time its sides had numerous registers (horizontal pictorial carvings) depicting scenes from the life of the pharaoh. It is 67 feet high and weighs 122 tons.

    It stands in the middle of a small archaeological square in what was Heliopolis. In this once-great city, eight of the 15 obelisks currently standing outside of Egypt were originally raised. Today the area is a suburb of Cairo.[1]
11. *New city of El Alamein.* It was initially raised in the reign of Ramses II (1279–13 BCE) in Pi-Ramesses, near the Nile Delta. It was later moved to Tanis, the capital city of Ramesses. Until modern times, Cairo had no obelisk, so in 1958 it was decided to move this

one in Tanis to Gezira, which is an island in the Nile between Giza and Cairo. The obelisk, which was in fragments, was restored, and a missing piece was added. It was located in the Al Andalus Garden, which had been created there for the obelisk. It stayed there for sixty years, until 2019, when it was moved to the new city of El Alamein, which is currently being developed on the Mediterranean coast sixty-five miles west of Alexandria. It was moved there in order to enhance the reputation of the new town. It is forty-four feet high, weighs ninety tons, and bears inscriptions in praise of the military prowess of Ramesses.[2]

II: ANCIENT EGYPTIAN OBELISKS IN MUSEUMS

There are several small Egyptian obelisks in various museums as parts of Egyptology collections. Such obelisks were not a part of my odyssey. Museums are man-made spaces built to display objects. Since my goal was to include only those obelisks that are standing outdoors in the "real world" to see what they are saying to their surroundings and to us, these museum obelisks were by definition outside my purpose. There are many small obelisk fragments in many museums, but this list includes only those that are relatively whole and intact. I have personally seen numbers 1 and 3.

1. *In London (in the British Museum[3]).* Here there are three obelisks on display. The first two are a pair of obelisks created by the last ethnic Egyptian pharaoh, Nectanebo II (358–340 BCE), for the temple complex

in the central Egyptian city of Hermopolis. Their upper halves are missing, and they now stand at nine feet each. They are unique in that they are composed of siltstone and are very dark in color, almost black. They are dedicated to Thoth, the chief god of Hermopolis. They stand in the Great Court of the Museum.

They were first mentioned in modern times in the eighteenth century by European travelers to Cairo. In 1798, the French scholars accompanying Napoleon to Egypt moved them to Alexandria with the intention to move them to the Louvre. Instead, when the British defeated the French at the Battle of the Nile, they seized the obelisks, the Rosetta Stone, and other artifacts and moved them to the British Museum.

The third obelisk in the museum comes from the time of Hatshepsut in the early 1400s BCE. Standing at about 5.5 feet, it is made of pink granite and was found in a Nubian town called Qasr Ibrim. The sign in the museum says the following: "On one side it is inscribed with the names of the queen described as 'beloved of Horus, Lord of Miam (modern-day Aniba), living forever like Ra.' The names were later erased as an attempt to remove her memory from history."

2. *In Durham, England (in the Oriental Museum).* A seven-foot obelisk from the reign of Amenhotep II (1227–01 BCE) is displayed there. It is one of a pair, the other being in the Nubian museum in Aswan (only a fragment there).
3. *In Aswan (in the Nubian Museum).* Two intact obelisks are there. They are a pair originally located in a chapel

near Abu Simbel and date to the reign of Ramesses II (1279–13 BCE). Both are eight feet tall. One is outside in a garden; the other is inside.

4. *In Poland (in the Poznań Archaeological Museum).* It is composed of granite and stands at ten feet tall and weighs 1.8 tons. It was raised during the reign of Ramesses II (1279–13 BCE) in the town of about thirty-five miles north of Cairo. It was brought to the Berlin Museum in 1896, its permanent home now. It has been on loan to Poznan for an extensive period.[4]

III: ANCIENT PSEUDO-EGYPTIAN OBELISKS: THE ROMAN EMPIRE

There are nine Roman-era obelisks currently standing in the lands of the former empire. They were closely modeled after Egyptian obelisks, primarily by Roman emperors, and are sometimes called "pseudo-Egyptian." Although dates are not always certain, three seem to have been transported or sited during the reign of Domitian (66–99 CE) and two (perhaps three) during the reign of Hadrian (117–138 CE). Domitian, who has been described as ruthless but effective, viewed the monoliths as a symbol of his divine right to rule. Hadrian's interest in obelisks was motivated more out of a fascination with all things Egyptian. His villa at Tivoli outside of Rome includes a building modeled after the Canopus with a little lake behind it having statues of several Egyptian gods surrounding it.

Here are the nine. They are all outdoors in public places, many in highly trafficked areas. I have personally seen all but number 8.

1. *Rome: on the Esquiline Hill.* This obelisk is uninscribed; hence its exact pedigree is not known with

certainty. In the first century CE, a Roman emperor, probably Domitian, moved it to Rome and raised it at the tomb of Augustus. It was found in three fragments there in 1519. In 1587 Pope Sixtus V had it restored and erected in the square on the Esquiline Hill behind the Basilica of Santa Maria Maggiore, which is one of the principal churches of Rome and a UNESCO World Heritage Site. It is made of Aswan red granite, stands forty-five feet tall, and weighs forty tons.

2. *Rome: on the Quirinal Hill.* This is one of a pair with the Esquiline obelisk. It too is uninscribed and was probably brought to Rome by Domitian and erected at the tomb of Caesar Augustus. Like its mate, it was found in fragments there. It was not until the reign of Pope Pius VI (1772–99) that it was repaired and re-erected on the Quirinal Hill in front of a papal summer home. Today the home, called the Quirinale Palace, is the residence of the President of Italy.

   It is positioned in the Piazza del Quirinale between two beautifully restored giant sculptures, possibly of Greek origin, called the Horse Tamers. It fronts the Scuderie, which was formerly a horse stable and is now the site of some of Rome's finest art exhibition spaces. Composed of Aswan red granite, the monolith stands forty-five feet tall and weighs forty-three tons.

3. *Rome: in the Piazza Navona.* It is red granite and quarried in Aswan on the orders of Emperor Domitian, who then moved it to the Iseum. On the shaft is Domitian depicted in the garb of a pharaoh, making him the sole emperor to have been so portrayed. First erected in the Iseum around 95 CE, it was moved to a Circus outside

of Rome on the Via Appia in 310 CE by the emperor Maxentius. It was toppled and lay in fragments until the seventeenth century, when Pope Innocent X moved it to the Piazza Navona, which itself had been a circus in ancient times. It was erected there in 1647.

This is one of the most famous obelisks in Rome for two reasons. First, the Piazza Navona is one of the major gathering spots in the city. Second, Bernini's extremely popular Fountain of the Four Rivers serves as its pedestal. The fountain is an allegory of the four continents Asia, Africa, Europe, and America, with beautifully sculpted symbols of the mighty rivers of each.

It is fifty-four feet high and weighs eighty-four tons.

4. *Rome: The Pincio.* This was quarried in Aswan by Hadrian in order to honor his dead lover Antonius, the Greek youth who drowned in Egypt. There are various accounts of the drowning. Some say it was accidental. Others say he was sacrificed to the gods in return for good health for Hadrian. In any event, Hadrian raised this obelisk as a tribute to him in Egypt around 130 CE. The location was in Antinoopolis, the town Hadrian founded in honor of the youth.

   At some point it was moved to Rome and was found buried in fragments during the pontificate of Urban VII (1623–44) near the church of Santa Croce in Gerusalemme. It changed hands several times until 1822, when Pope Pius VII erected it on Monte Pincio, which is in the middle of the park we today call the Villa Borghese.

   It is thirty feet high and weighs eighteen tons. Its inscription pays tribute to Antonius. Its hieroglyphs are poorly shaped, which indicates they were cut by people (in this case, the Romans) with little knowledge of the Egyptian language.

5. *Rome: in front of the Church of the Trinita dei Monti atop the Spanish Steps (a.k.a. the Sallustiano obelisk).* It was quarried in Aswan in the first or second century CE, perhaps by a Roman emperor such as Hadrian or Aurelius, who both loved Egypt. It appears to be a copy of the Flaminio obelisk in the Piazza del Popolo, and the two have similar inscriptions. It has moved around Rome a few times since its original location in the Sallustiani Gardens on the Via Salaria. It was discovered in the ruins there. Originally intended to stand alongside the obelisk in front of St. John Lateran, it was finally erected in its current location in 1789 by Pope Pius VI. Its placement there was controversial. It was feared that the monolith would weaken the foundation of the church and also ruin the view from the top of the Spanish steps. Neither has occurred, and today it is one of the most iconic sights in Rome.

   The Church of Trinita dei Monti has been under French management since the sixteenth century. It and the nearby Villa Medici are considered part of the French state.

6. *Israel (in the ruins of the Roman port of Caesarea).* This obelisk was found in fragments in the 1980s in the ruins of a hippodrome in Caesarea. This port city was created in the reign of King Herod (37–4 BCE) when Judaea was part of the Roman Empire. It has no inscription, so its provenance is not known with certainty. It is probably a copy made by a Roman emperor, perhaps Hadrian.

It is thirty-nine feet high and weighs one hundred tons. It stands alone in an isolated area of Caesarea National Park.

7. *Arles, France.* This obelisk is uninscribed, and its exact provenance is unclear. It is likely made of granite from Aswan, but possibly from an unknown quarry outside of Egypt. Some experts think it was likely created in the fourth century CE by either Emperor Constantine I or his son Constantius II to stand in or near the hippodrome in Arles, which was then a town in the Roman province of Provinzia. It fell, was rediscovered in 1389, and was erected by Louis XIV in the seventeenth century.

   It is fifty feet tall and stands in front of the town hall. Nearby are a number of Roman monuments which are part of a UNESCO World Heritage Site.

8. *Benevento, Italy.* This obelisk was probably created by Domitian in the late first century CE as part of a pair for the Temple of Isis in Rome. It was found there in four pieces, reassembled, and moved to the Piazza Papiniano in Benevento, a small town forty miles northeast of Naples.

   It is an interesting monolith, because it has not only hieroglyphs on all four sides but also Latin and Greek inscriptions on the pedestal. It is known that Jean-François Champollion translated its hieroglyphs during the time he was decoding the Rosetta Stone. But it is not known if this obelisk and pedestal, because of its multi-language inscriptions, helped him solve the puzzle.

9. *The Walled Obelisk (Istanbul).* It is a Roman stone monument in the form of an obelisk that was originally erected

in the reign of the Roman Emperor Theodosius I (379–395 CE) or one of his immediate successors. It was badly damaged over time and was repaired extensively in the tenth century by Emperor Constantius VII and covered with brass plates. The brass was taken down and melted by the Crusaders in 1204. It was badly damaged by an earthquake in 1894 and was repaired again. It is 105 feet high and stands in the hippodrome in Sultanahmet Square along with the Obelisk of Theodosius and the Greek Serpentine column. See Chapter 13 for more context.

IV: OTHER ANCIENT PSEUDO-EGYPTIAN OBELISKS

Besides the Romans, several other ancient civilizations created obelisks. All were influenced by the Egyptians, who were trading partners with these other civilizations. Except for number 5, all of these obelisks are in museums. I have seen all but number 4 (I saw number 5 when it stood in Rome years ago).

1. *Assyrian: The Black Obelisk (in the British Museum).* It was erected in Nimrud (twenty miles south of Mosul in modern Iraq) around 825 BCE during the reign of the Assyrian King Shalmaneser III. It was discovered by a British archaeologist in 1843. On its surface are twenty relief scenes, five on each side, that represent five different conquered kings paying tribute to Shalmaneser.

   Its inscription is very significant. It is in Akkadian, which is the earliest Semitic language, and it uses the cuneiform script. It bears the first known reference to the Persians. Also it contains the first reference to a Biblical figure—Jehu, king of Israel.

It is 6.5 feet tall and made of black limestone. It is now in the British Museum next to the Assyrian White Obelisk. These are the only two intact Assyrian obelisks in the world.

2. *Assyrian: The White Obelisk (in the British Museum).* It was erected by either King Ashurnasirpal I (1020 BCE) or Ashurnasirpal II (around 870 BCE). This makes it the oldest surviving Assyrian obelisk. It was discovered in Nineveh (Mosul in modern Iraq) in 1853 by an Iraqi archaeologist. It is made of white limestone and is 9.3 feet tall. In it are engravings of military campaigns, hunting, and the king offering a gift to the goddess Ishtar, the principal deity of Nineveh. It stands next to the Black Obelisk in the British Museum.
3. *Phoenician (in Beirut).* It was created during the reign of the Phoenician king Abishemu I (1800 BCE). It is the oldest obelisk outside of Egypt in the world. It is inscribed in Egyptian hieroglyphs. It was discovered by the French archaeologist Maurice Dunand in 1950 in the ruins of Byblos on the coast of modern Lebanon. It was found in the remains of a temple which Dunand named the Temple of the Obelisks because a number of "obelisks" were found there. This is the only complete obelisk with a pyramidion found in the Temple of the Obelisks. It is 4.7 feet tall, made of white limestone, and is now on display in the National Museum of Beirut.

The Temple of the Obelisks was not open to visitors when I visited Lebanon in 2019. However, Byblos is fascinating and well worth a visit. It is one of the oldest cities in the world and has many historical attractions dating back to the Phoenicians to Crusader times to the Ottomans to the present. The entire coast of Lebanon is of great historic interest. Beirut lies twenty-five miles south, and just south of Beirut lie the cities of Sidon and Tyre. Tyre is twelve miles north of the border with Israel and is the place from which the Phoenicians who founded Carthage set sail. Both Sidon and Tyre are mentioned in the Bible as places Jesus visited.

4. *Nubian (in Khartoum, Sudan).* In the eighth century BCE, the Nubian kingdom of Kush conquered Egypt. The Kushite ruler King Piye was the first pharaoh of the twenty-fifth dynasty (747–56 BCE). Many Nubian obelisks that imitated those of the Egyptians were created. The only one that is substantially intact is made of black granite and is standing today in the National Museum in Khartoum. It is sometimes referred to as the Obelisk of Piye.
5. *Ethiopian (In Axum).* It is sometimes considered more of a stele (stone monument) than an obelisk. Created in the fourth century CE, it is found in the historic Ethiopian city of Aksum (now called Axum) along with many other stelae of the same era. It is seventy-nine feet tall and composed of a single block of stone derived from Ethiopian igneous rock called phonolite. It has false doors carved into its base.

   It was created by King Ezana (321–360 CE), who became a Christian. It stood untoppled until 1937, when Mussolini invaded Ethiopia and moved it to Rome. There it remained until 2005 when Italy finally moved it back to Ethiopia, Italy paying for the move. It was reassembled and re-erected in Axum in 2008. I drove past this obelisk many times in Rome before it was moved. It stood near the Circus Maximus in front of FAO (the UN Headquarters for Food and Agriculture).

V: SOME FAMOUS MODERN OBELISKS

There are many impressive obelisk-like modern buildings. In fact you could say that all skyscrapers are to some degree the direct descendants of the Egyptian obelisk. But I'll restrict myself to mentioning only a few that have special significance and were built with the stated purpose of echoing their Egyptian architectural ancestor.

1. *Boston. Bunker Hill Monument.* It is the first major obelisk memorial in the United States. It was built to honor the men who fought in the Battle of Bunker Hill, a famous battle of the American Revolutionary War. In 1822, a twenty-two-year-old Boston sculptor named Horatio Greenough, using the obelisk in front of St. John Lateran in Rome as his inspiration, won a design competition for the monument. Simon Willard was appointed architect and supervised the project. It was completed and dedicated in 1843 with President Taylor in attendance. Daniel Webster delivered the commemoratory speech.

   Composed of granite from the quarries of Quincy, Massachusetts, it weighs 7,000 tons, stands at 221 feet, and has 297 steps (all of which were once climbed by yours truly with his five-year-old daughter on his shoulders when he was a far younger man).

The new Leonard P. Zakim Bunker Hill Memorial Bridge (completed in 2003) is nearby, spanning the Charles River, connecting Charlestown with Cambridge. It is the widest cable-stayed bridge in the world. Its cables are attached to two cradles, the tops of which are in the form of obelisks to reflect the shape of the nearby Bunker Hill Memorial. When one is approaching the city from the north, the bridge and the Bunker Hill monument together offer what may be the most obelisk-centric entry into any city in the United States—maybe the world.

2. *The Washington Monument (Washington, DC).* At 555 feet, it is the tallest obelisk in the world. In fact, at one point it was the tallest building of any type in the world. The Pyramid at Giza (2570 BCE), at a height of 481 feet, was the tallest building for over 3,800 years, until the Cathedral at Lincoln (UK) was built in 1311 with a spire reaching 525 feet. In 1548, however, it collapsed and was never rebuilt. Cologne cathedral, at a height of 515 feet, then became the tallest building. When the Washington Monument was finished in 1885, it then became the tallest building in the world. It has a hollowed-out core. Interestingly, this obelisk was designed by the architect Robert Mills in 1836. He had also proposed an obelisk design for the Bunker Hill Monument years earlier, but his design was rejected for a simpler obelisk design of Horatio Greenough as noted above.

■ ■ ■

KEY DATES AND PEOPLE IN OBELISK HISTORY: THE BIG PICTURE

The Egyptian people are a unique ethnicity. Although their official language is Arabic, they are not Arabs. They adopted that language when they were conquered by the Arabs in the seventh century CE. At that point, their language, Coptic, started to become extinct. No one speaks it today, and its only real presence in Egyptian life is in the liturgy of the Coptic Christians. A recent series of DNA tests have shown that over 75 percent of all Egyptians alive today are direct descendants of the ancient Egyptians dating back to the time of the obelisks.

The history of Ancient Egypt can be broken down into the following periods:

- Predynastic Period: Before 3150 BCE. Egypt divided into Upper and Lower Egypt
- Early Dynastic: 3150–2686 BCE. Unification of Upper and Lower Egypt.
- Old Kingdom: 2686–2181 BCE. Great Pyramids and Sphinx built at Giza.
- First Intermediate Period: 2181–2055 BCE. Egypt splits into two smaller states.
- Middle Kingdom: 2134–1690 BCE. First obelisk erected at Heliopolis by Senusret I.
- Second Intermediate Period: 1674–1549 BCE. Hyksos people seize power in north.
- New Kingdom: 1549–1069 BCE. Era of greatest Egyptian power and strongest leaders.
- Third Intermediate Period: 1069–653 BCE. Egypt falls under Nubian and Lybian rule.

- Late Period: 664–332 BCE. Egypt regains throne.
- Ptolemaic Period: 332–30 BCE. Alexander the Great and then his general Ptolemy and successors rule.
- Roman Period: 30 BCE–395 CE.

The Pharaonic history of Egypt spans over 3,100 years and 30 distinct dynasties. The first dynasty began in 3150 BCE with the Pharaoh Narmer (also called Menes) and ended with the death of its last ruler, Cleopatra, in 30 BCE.

Below are the key players in the history of the twenty-six Egyptian obelisks standing today.

KEY PHARAOHS

All told, Egypt had 170 pharaohs, starting with Narmer (also called Menes) in 3150 BCE and ending with Cleopatra VII in 30 BCE. Regarding obelisk creation, here are the most important:

- *Senusret I (Middle Kingdom, 12th Dynasty, 1971–1926 BCE).* Set up the two oldest surviving obelisks around 1950 BCE, one in Heliopolis and the other in Faiyum, Egypt.
- *Hatshepsut (New Kingdom, 18th Dynasty, 1507–1458 BCE).* Second female pharaoh (Sobekneferu, who died in 1802 BCE, is generally considered to be the first). Set up obelisk in Luxor at Temple of Karnak. She commissioned the largest obelisk of all time, but it lies unfinished in the bedrock in its quarry in Aswan.
- *Thutmose III (New Kingdom, 18th Dynasty, 1479–1425 BCE).* Another powerful leader. Ordered four obelisks that are still standing, including the

tallest one in the world now at the church of St. John Lateran in Rome and Cleopatra's Needles, now in London and New York.

- *Ramesses II (New Kingdom, 19th Dynasty, 1279–1213).* Considered to be the most powerful of all the 170 pharaohs, he also set up the most obelisks. Fragments of twenty-three have been found in his capital city of Tanis alone. Six are still standing today in various parts of the world.
- *Apries (Late Period, 26th Dynasty, 586–570 BCE).* Erected two obelisks that are still standing. He is also called Hophra.
- *Akhenaten (New Kingdom, 18th Dynasty, 1353–1336 BCE, formerly known as Amenhotep IV).* The probable father of King Tutankhamen, he erected no obelisks. Sometimes called the "heretic pharaoh," he is a significant figure because he rejected the traditional polytheism of Egyptian religion and proclaimed Aten, the god of the solar disc, as the one supreme god and the creator of all things. He is considered today to be the founder of monotheism, and his writings were known to the Jews.

KEY EGYPTIAN GODS

A number of gods are associated with obelisks and often have their names inscribed on them. The most prominent are the following:

- *Ra.* God of sun and light. He is usually depicted with a red sun disc. Interestingly, some scholars believe that the sun in ancient Egypt was literally red, not yellow, because of all of the dust particles in the air.

- *Amun-Ra*. Created the world, patron of Theban pharaohs in particular. Karnak was his temple.
- *Atum*. God of the evening sun.
- *Isis*. Giver of life, protector of the kingdom from enemies, possessed magical powers of healing. She was widely worshipped in the Greco-Roman world as well.
- *Horus*. God of kings, had the head of a falcon.
- *Osiris*. God of fertility, the afterlife, the dead, and resurrection. He was married to Isis.

OTHER KEY FIGURES IN OBELISK HISTORY

- *Alexander the Great*. The Greek Macedonian who at the age of twenty-five, in 332 BCE, conquered Egypt and the Persians and established his headquarters at a new northern city he named Alexandria. When he died, his vast kingdom was divided into three parts, with each governed by former generals in his army. The Egyptian territory was governed by general Ptolemy Sotar, who became Pharaoh Ptolemy I.
- *The Ptolemies*. The twelve pharaohs who composed the Ptolemaic Dynasty. The dynasty lasted 310 years. These pharaohs were all ethnic Greek.
- *Julius Caesar*. Subjugated Egypt in 48 BCE, making it a part of the Roman Empire. It was Rome's biggest trading partner and home to essential products like cotton.
- *Mark Antony*. With Lepidus and Pompey, he formed the first Triumvirate that succeeded Julius Caesar. He

later became the sole Roman ruler of Egypt. He was subsequently defeated by Octavian and committed suicide in 30 BCE.

- *Cleopatra.* Officially Cleopatra VII, she was the last Egyptian pharaoh of all time. She, along with Mark Antony, was defeated by Octavian and committed suicide. Both Caesar (with whom she had a child) and Mark Antony were her lovers.
- *Caesar Augustus (Octavian).* Defeated Antony and Cleopatra at the Battle of Actium in 30 BCE. Became first coruler, then sole ruler of the empire. He began the practice of Europeans moving the obelisks to Rome in 13 BCE.
- *Theodosius.* The Roman emperor who, in 341 CE, moved an obelisk to the new eastern capital of the Roman Empire, Constantinople.
- *Pope Sixtus V.* The "obelisk pope." He sought out obelisks fallen and buried in Rome and raised them in new locations for the greater glory of God and the Catholic Church. He also launched a number of new construction projects in the city. He was a leader of the Counter Reformation and excommunicated both Queen Elizabeth of England and Henry IV of France. His reign as pope was relatively brief (1585–90), given his significant impact.
- *Napoleon.* With the goal of establishing France as a global empire to rival that of England, he invaded Egypt in 1798. Besides large numbers of troops, he brought with him 167 scholars of all types to study Egyptian civilization, which had been neglected for centuries. Although he was defeated militarily by the British and

Ottomans, he set off a worldwide fascination with all things Egyptian. This so-called Egyptomania lasted throughout the nineteenth century.

- *Jean-François Champollion.* The French archaeologist who is credited with translating the Rosetta Stone.
- *William John Bankes.* The English polymath who contributed to the translation of the Rosetta Stone.
- *Muhammad Ali.* The Ottoman governor of Egypt and de facto leader of the country in the early 1800s. He gifted an obelisk to France and one to England. Prior to that, numerous obelisks had been taken from Egypt by Roman emperors in ancient times. None of them were gifted.

LIST OF ILLUSTRATIONS

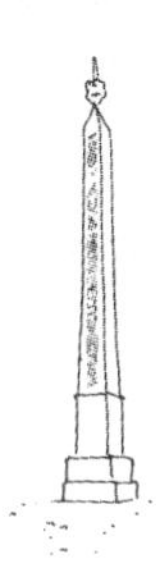

BIBLIOGRAPHY

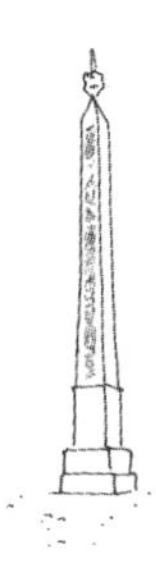

My goal has not been to conduct extensive primary research on the obelisks. Many experts are doing that. My interest has been to offer reflections on Egyptian obelisks in their modern contexts based on personal site visits. At these sites, signage and on-site guides communicated to me an incredible amount of useful information, with Wikipedia often providing a quick secondary verification of basic historical background and facts. For deeper dives into the history of some of the obelisks and relevant Egyptian history, I recommend the following:

Curran, Brian. A., Anthony Grafton, Pamela O. Long, and Benjamin Weiss. *Obelisk: A History*. The Burndy Library, 2009.

Dolnick, Edward. *The Writing of the Gods*. Simon and Schuster, 2021.

Edsel, Robert. *Saving Italy*. W. W. Norton, 2014.

Habachi, Labib. *The Obelisks of Egypt: Skyscrapers of the Past*. Charles Scribner's Sons, 1977.

Olson, Lynne. *Empress of the Nile*. Random House, 2023.

Sebba, Anne. *The Exiled Collector: William Bankes and the Making of an English Country House*. Dovecote Press, 2022.

Sorek, Susan. *Cleopatra's Needles*. Bristol Phoenix Press, 2010.

NOTES

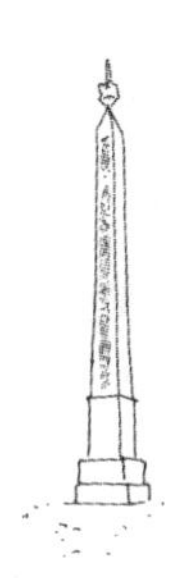

PROLOGUE

1. "History of Early American Landscape Design," by Robyn Asleson, a project of the Center for Advanced Study in the Visual Arts, National Gallery of Art, accessed January 23, 2024, https://heald.nga.gov/mediawiki/index.php/Bunker_Hill_Monument#History.

CHAPTER 1

1. *The Third Man*, British Lion Films, 1949.

CHAPTER 2

1. Herodotus, *The Histories* (London: Penguin Classics, 1954), 86–153.
2. Mark Twain, *The Innocents Abroad* (New York: Modern Library, 2003), 458–476.
3. "Orson Welles' Vienna," https://www.youtube.com/watch?v=6kz39VdxoQc&ab_channel=MattBC, accessed January 23, 2024. From the text in the video: "In 1968 and 1969, Orson Welles spent time in Europe filming segments for a TV special, initially called Orson's Bag, then One-Man Band. One episode was filmed in Vienna,

filmed partially on location . . . the material was left by Welles as a working print, completely edited and partly mixe."

4. Twain, 458–476.

CHAPTER 3

1. *The Tonight Show*, starring Johnny Carson, NBC.
2. Joanna Kavenna, *The Ice Museum: In Search of the Lost Land of Thule* (New York, Viking Adult, 2006).

PART II

1. For a detailed overview of Napoleon's exploits in Egypt, see Edward Dolnick, *The Writing of the Gods* (New York, Scribner, 2021).

CHAPTER 4

1. For more detailed descriptions of the facts surrounding the Central Park Obelisk, see Brian Curran et al., *Obelisk: A History* (Cambridge, Ma., The Burndy Library 2009), 271–278. See also Jessica Sain-Baird, "How the Obelisk Made Its Home in Central Park," *Magazine of Central Park Conservancy*, February 1, 2018.
2. Nathaniel Hawthorne, *The Scarlet Letter* (New York, Modern Library, 200), 11. The full quote is as follows: "Human nature will not flourish, any more than a potato, if it be planted and replanted, for too long a series of generations, in the same worn-out soil. My children have had other birthplaces, and, so far as their fortunes may be within my control, shall strike their roots into unaccustomed earth."

CHAPTER 5

1. For more details on the Paris obelisk, see Brian Curran et al., *Obelisk: A History*, 242–255.
2. *The Federalist Papers*, Federalist No. 1, The Project Gutenberg eBook of The Federalist Papers (Release date 1991). Regarding the speeches at the Constitutional Convention warning of demagogues, see Eli Merritt, "Civics 101: Keep Demagogues Out of Democracy," *The Vanderbilt Project on Unity and American Democracy*, April 7, 2021, https://www.vanderbilt.edu/unity/2021/04/07/civics-101-keep-demagogues-out-of-democracy.

CHAPTER 6

1. For more detail on the London obelisk, see Susan Sorek, *Cleopatra's Needles* (Exeter: Bristol Phoenix Press, 2008), 124–130, and Curran et al., *Obelisk: A History*, 257–67.
2. London Walks conducts daily guided walking tours on dozens of topics. See them at www.walks.com.
3. For an account of the transfer, see *The Egyptian Independent*, August 9, 2019.

CHAPTER 7

1. The contribution of Bankes and his obelisk to the translation of the Rosetta Stone is described by Edward Dolnick in *The Writing of the Gods*, 147–153.
2. For more on the Rosetta Mission and *Philae* lander, see the abstract on this subject called "The Philae Lander and Mission Overview" published by The Royal Society Publishing, May 29, 2017, https://royalsocietypublishing.org/doi/10.1098/rsta.2016.0248.
3. Anne Sebba, *The Exiled Collector: William Bankes and the Making of an English Country House* (Stanbridge, Wimborne Minster: Dovecote Press, 2022).
4. For visits to Kingston Lacy, see www.nationaltrust.org.uk.

CHAPTER 8

1. *Cambridge Ancient History,* Volume 10, Cambridge University Press. 1996.
2. For a fuller explanation of Augustus's imperial ambitions and posturings as manifested in these two obelisks, see Curran et al., *Obelisk: A History*, 37–40, and Sorek, *Cleopatra's Needles*, 45–56.
3. As quoted in the movie *Patton,* 20th Century Fox, 1970.
4. Sorek, *Cleopatra's Needles*, 73.
5. BBC News, "Obelisk Arrives Back in Ethiopia," April 19, 2005, http://news.bbc.co.uk/2/hi/africa/4458105.stm.
6. Maurice Finocchiaro, editor and translator, *The Galileo Affair* (Berkeley, CA: University of California Press, 1989).

CHAPTER 9

1. For more on the history and the logistics of the Vatican obelisk, see Sorek, *Cleopatra's Needles*, 60–69, and Curran et al., *Obelisk: A History*, 103.
2. For the parallels between Psalm 104 and the Hymn to Aten, see www.factsaboutreligion.com, www.intertextual.com, and www.thetorah.com.
3. Laurie Goodstein, "An Evangelizer on the Right, With His Eye on the Future," *New York Times*, April 19, 2005, https://www.nytimes.com/2005/04/20/world/worldspecial2/an-evangelizer-on-the-rightwith-his-eye-on-the-future.html.
4. For more on the Lateran Obelisk, see Sorek, *Cleopatra's Needles*, 101–106, and Curran et al., *Obelisk: A History*, 136–37.

CHAPTER 10

1. For more on the Rotonda obelisk, see Sorek, *Cleopatra's Needles*, 77.
2. For more on the elephant obelisk, see Curran et al., *Obelisk: A History*, 171–2.
3. For more on the Mattei obelisk, see Sorek, *Cleopatra's Needles*, 78.
4. For more on the Center for American Studies, see www.centrostudiamericani.org.
5. There is debate as to the origin of this quote. It is usually attributed to Twain, and in 1999 it appeared on a widely distributed poster for Peace Corps recruitment.

CHAPTER 11

1. For more on the Boboli obelisk, see Samuel Oer de Almeida, "The Boboli Obelisk—A Monument in Motion," *European Heritage Times*, 2022, https://www.europeanheritagetimes.eu/2021/05/21/the-boboli-obelisk-a-monument-in-motion.
2. *Encyclopedia Britannica Online*, s.v. "Etruscan Language," https://www.britannica.com/topic/Etruscan-language/Grammatical-characteristics, accessed January 23, 2024. "Since the language is undeciphered, meaning can be assigned with certainty to only a few Etruscan words that occur very infrequently in the texts." See also Dolnick, *The Writing of the Gods*, 21. Dolnick writes of the Etruscan language, "Scholars have learned to read the script of the Etruscans,

who built a thriving culture in Italy centuries before the Romans. But they did not know what the sounds meant. In effect, they can read sounds aloud, but they do not know if they have read *To be or not to be* or *All cats love Frisky Nibbles*."

3. Poetry Foundation, "Ode on a Grecian Urn by John Keats," n.d., https://www.poetryfoundation.org/poems/44477/ode-on-a-grecian-urn.
4. World Heritage Convention, whc.unesco.org.
5. For more on the Urbino obelisk, see Sorek, *Cleopatra's Needles*, 58.
6. See also "Federico da Montefeltro," Wikipedia, last modified October 24, 2023, https://en.wikipedia.org/wiki/Federico_da_Montefeltro.
7. *The Court Jester*, Paramount Pictures, 1955. To hear Kaye's classic tongue twister in its entirety, search for "The Pellet with the Poison" on YouTube.
8. For more information on Pasquale Rotondi, see Robert Edsel, *Saving Italy* (New York, W.W. Norton, 2014), 113–115, 138, 147.

CHAPTER 12

1. For more on the Baha'i faith, see J. S. Esslemont, *Baha'U'llah and the New Era: An Introduction to the Baha'i Faith* (Wilmette, Illinois: Baha'i Publishing Trust, 1970) and Jason Boyett, *12 Major World Religions* (Berkeley, Zephyros Press, 2016).
2. This quote is from Wordsworth's 1807 sonnet titled "The World Is Too Much With Us." In it he laments that the Industrial Revolution has ushered in a world that is too materialistic and too distanced from nature.

CHAPTER 13

1. The following are good sources of information on these obelisks: Labib Habachi, *The Obelisks of Egypt, Skyscrapers of the Past* (New York, Charles Scribner's Sons, 1977), 145–151; E. A. Wallis Budge, *Cleopatra's Needles and Other Egyptian Obelisks* (London: The Religious Tract Society, 1926) 160–165; Editors of the Madain Project, "Walled Obelisk," https://madainproject.com/walled_obelisk, accessed January 23, 2024.

CHAPTER 14

1. Herodotus, *The Histories*, by Herodotus (London, Penguin Classics, 1954), 386-87.
2. George Eliot, *Middlemarch* (New York, Barnes and Noble Classics edition, 2003) 794.
3. Homer, *The Odyssey* (London, Penguin Deluxe Classic Edition, 1996). Books 22–24.
4. Alfred Lord Tennyson, "Ulysses."
5. *Ithaca*, by Constantine Cavafy, translated by Edmund Keeley/Philip Sherrard, https://www.greeka.com/ionian/ithaca/about/poem/.

AFTERWORD

1. Information on two of the Egyptian obelisks I personally did not see (Faiyum and Heliopolis) can be found on Wikipedia.
2. For more details on the background and new location of the obelisk at New City of El-Alamein, see the websites of *Egypt Today,* August 8, 2019 (www.egypttoday.com) and *The Egypt Independent*, August 9, 2019 (www.egyptindependent.com).
3. For more information on the obelisks in the British Museum, see the museum's website at www.britishmuseum.org/research/.collection_online/.aspx.
4. Information on the Durham (durham.ac.uk/things-to-do/venues/oriental-museum) and Poznan (http://www.obelisks.org/en/poznan.htm) obelisks can be found online.

ACKNOWLEDGMENTS

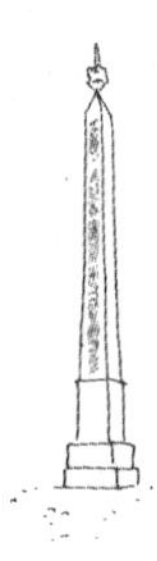

This book never would have happened had I not made a trip to Egypt with two people: my son-in-law, Dana Snyder, and my friend Qaisar Shareef. Aside from being great travel companions, they have both been extremely supportive of this entire project, offering their input along the way. Also, Qaisar, who is a published author and accomplished blogger on a variety of issues in the news, spent much time sharing his experiences in publishing with me, which proved to be absolutely essential. His careful reading of my manuscript was immensely helpful. Thanks, Q!!

The Egypt trip only came together when Dana connected us to Gus Gleiter, the owner of Egypt Adventures Travel. Gus listened to our crazy plan, made sense of it, and made it happen. He worked with Lulu of LuluHolidays in Egypt, who provided the guides and boots-on-the-ground support we needed. The entire team was wonderful, and I recommend them highly to anyone interested in a small, customized, and affordable trip to Egypt. Gus can be reached at gus@egyptadventurestravel.com.

I want to thank all of the people who took the time to read portions of my manuscript and provide much useful feedback. This includes Wally Murray, Stefano Dodero, Pat Kiernan (who gave me the phrase "fun with a purpose"), Patrick Spear, John Galantic, Fred and Diane L'Ecuyer, and the Pittsburgh crew of Pete Lucey, Jon Klemens, Joe Schramm. Every one of you gave me an idea for how to make what you read better. I'd also like to thank of the National Parks Service in Boston, specifically David Vecchioli, Ethan Beeler, and Patrick Boyce, who all gave me useful perspective on the Bunker Hill Monument/Obelisk. The Parks Service is a great organization with personnel who are always informed and committed.

It's difficult for a first-time author to understand the publishing world, and several people in addition to Qaisar helped me in that regard. My friend and kindred spirit Michael Wright, the director of European Programs at Duquesne University helped me get useful input from industry experts. My friend and business mentor, Dan Harris, a published author of five books, offered me encouragement as well as useful perspective on both writing and publishing. Special thanks go to my friend and business colleague Trey Holder, who introduced me to Naren Aryal, CEO of Amplify Publishing. Naren and all the team at Amplify are true professionals and provided all the support I could ever hope for. I am deeply grateful to them all, especially to my editor, Brand Coward, who rolled up his sleeves and coached me through every step of the publishing process. A true pro in every sense of the word and, even better, a super person to work with.

But above all, I thank my wonderful family. Each of my four daughters—Christine, Caroline, Michelle, and Amanda—were so encouraging (and probably a bit amused and perhaps baffled) regarding their father's quixotic literary undertaking. They have all inspired me every day of their lives, whether they know it or not. Christine also played a major role in preparing the manuscript in a professional format that I just didn't have the skills to do myself.

And then there's my wife, Eileen. We've traveled the world together—sometimes against her better judgment! But she has done it and continues to do so. And her sketches are really wonderful! I am fully—and happily—aware that they often capture the spirit and intent of the book better than my words do. There's not a thing I've done since we met that she hasn't made better.

ABOUT THE AUTHOR

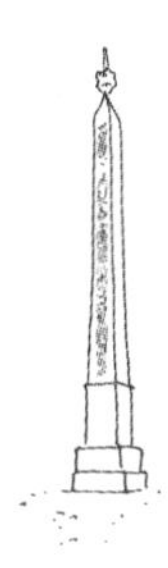

MARK CICCONE is a semi-retired world traveler who worked for thirty-two years in various senior management positions at Procter & Gamble, where he traveled widely in the US and abroad, including a stint living in Italy.

He subsequently became a consultant with Monitor (now Monitor Deloitte) in Cambridge, Massachusetts, and then the president of a boutique consulting firm specializing in strategy and innovation.

He holds bachelor's and master's degrees from Duquesne University in Pittsburgh, where he has taught twice: once as a graduate student in English and, more recently, as an instructor in the business school at the university's campus in Rome.

He lives in the suburbs of Boston with his wife, Eileen. They have four daughters and one granddaughter. His hobbies include travel, history, skiing, and following the Boston sports teams.

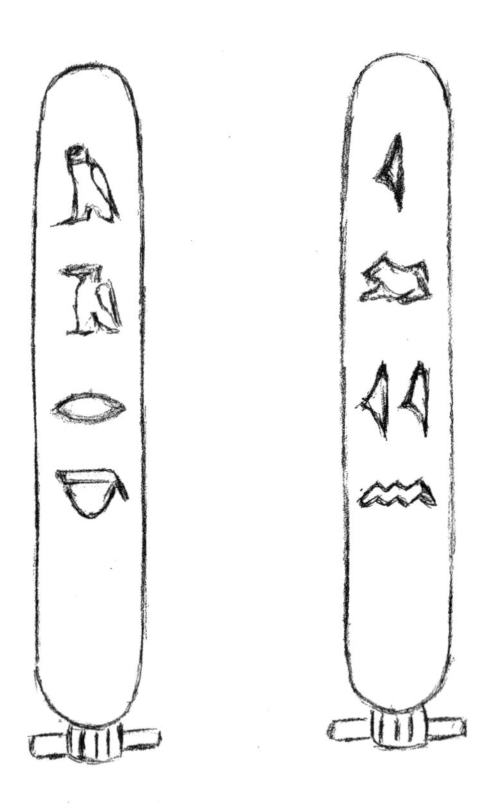

M	Owl
A	Vulture
R	Mouth
K	Basket

Ī	Reed
L	Lion
Ē	Two Reeds
N	Water